# BrightRED Study Guide

## Curriculum for Excellence

## N5

# COMPUTING SCIENCE

Alan Williams

BrightRED
PUBLISHING

First published in 2013 by:
**Bright Red Publishing Ltd**
**1 Torphichen Street**
**Edinburgh**
**EH3 8HX**

Reprinted with corrections 2013 and 2015. New edition published 2017.

A CIP record for this book is available from the British Library

ISBN 978-1-84948-311-7

With thanks to:
PDQ Digital Media, Bungay (layout), Ivor Normand (editorial)
Cover design and series book design by Caleb Rutherford – e i d e t i c

*Acknowledgements*
Every effort has been made to seek all copyright-holders. If any have been overlooked, then Bright Red Publishing will be delighted to make the necessary arrangements. All internet links in the text were correct at the time of going to press.

Permission has been sought from all relevant copyright-holders. Bright Red Publishing are grateful for the use of the following:

Konstantin Chagin/Shutterstock.com (p 6); several images licensed by Ingram Image (pages 9, 17, 18, 19, 22, 28, 30, 40, 42, 44, 50, 55, 60, 61, 69, 75, 76, 79, 80, 84, 86); Petr koya979/Shutterstock.com (p 11); cobrasoft/Stock-Xchnge (p 12); Stephen Coburn/ Shutterstock.com (p 14); jcjgphotography/Shutterstock.com (p 15); giel/Stock-Xchnge (p 16); grafvision/Shutterstock.com (p 20); wavebreakmedia/Shutterstock.com (p 21); 621st Contingency Response Wing/CreativeCommons (CC BY 2.0)[1] (p 24); Andi Collington (p 27); Vaclavek/Shutterstock.com (p 34); sebleedelisle/CreativeCommons (CC BY 2.0)[1] (p 37); Stock-Xchnge (p 38); screenshot of 'Flying Toasters' screensaver, After Dark software © Berkeley Systems (p 41); screenshot used with permission from Microsoft (p 41); gemphoto/Shutterstock.com (p 42); Stoppe/Creative Commons (CC0 1.0) (p 48); Garsya/Shutterstock.com (p 53); Caleb Rutherford (p 56); Horia Varlan/Creative Commons (CC BY 2.0)[1] (p 70); cstrom/Creative Commons (CC BY-SA 2.0)[2] (p 70); Denis Tabler/ Shutterstock.com (p 80); Image © Vodafone Limited (p 81); monokini/freeimages.com (p 85); Alexander Ermolaev/Shutterstock.com (p 88); Robyn Mackenzie/Shutterstock.com (p 89); Andresr/Shutterstock.com (p 90); Ron and Joe/Shutterstock.com (p 90); ostill/ Shutterstock.com (p 93).

[1](CC BY 2.0) http://creativecommons.org/licenses/by/2.0/
[2](CC BY-SA 2.0) http://creativecommons.org/licenses/by-sa/2.0/

Printed and bound in the UK.

# CONTENTS

## 1 THE NATIONAL 5 COURSE

## 2 SOFTWARE DESIGN AND DEVELOPMENT

## 3 COMPUTER SYSTEMS

## 4 DATABASE DESIGN AND DEVELOPMENT

## 5 WEB DESIGN AND DEVELOPMENT

## 6 COURSE ASSESSMENT

## 7 GLOSSARY

# SYLLABUS AND ASSESSMENT

## SYLLABUS

This course has four areas of study:

1 Software Design and Development
2 Computer Systems
3 Database Design and Development
4 Web Design and Development.

An outline of the contents of each area is given in the tables below.

| Software Design and Development | |
|---|---|
| Analysis | The phases of the development process: analysis, design, implementation, testing, documentation and evaluation. Functional requirements of a problem: input, processing and output. |
| Design notations | Structure diagrams      Pseudocode      Flowcharts |
| User interface design | Wireframes |
| Data types and structures | Character, string, integer, real, Boolean<br>1–D arrays |
| Computational constructs | Assigning values<br>Arithmetic operations (+, -, $^*$, /, ^)<br>Concatenate strings<br>Expressions to concatenate strings<br>Selection constructs using simple conditional statements with <, >, ≤, ≥, =, ≠ operators<br>Selection constructs using complex condition statements<br>Logical operators (AND, OR, NOT)<br>Iteration using fixed and conditional loops<br>Pre-defined functions (with parameters): random, round, length |
| Standard algorithms | Input validation<br>Running total within loop<br>Traversing a 1-D array |
| Testing | Normal, extreme and exceptional test data<br>Syntax, execution and logic errors |
| Evaluation | Fitness for purpose<br>Efficient use of coding constructs<br>Robustness<br>Readability: internal commentary, meaningful identifiers, indentation, white space |

| Computer Systems | |
|---|---|
| Data representation | Binary to represent positive integers<br>Floating-point numbers<br>Convert from binary to decimal and vice versa<br>Extended ASCII code (8-bit) used to represent characters<br>Graphics (bit-mapped and vector) |
| Computer structure | Processor (registers, ALU, control unit)<br>Memory locations with unique addresses<br>Buses (data and address) |
| Translators | Translation of high-level program code into machine code with interpreters and compilers |
| Environmental impact | The impact of the energy use of computer systems on the environment<br>Measures to use less power |
| Security precautions | Firewalls      Encryption in electronic communications |

## ONLINE

This book is supported by the Bright Red Digital Zone. Visit www.brightredbooks.net/N5Computing

## DON'T FORGET

You should use the syllabus as a kind of checklist to make sure that you understand exactly what knowledge is required for assessments in this course. Read it through and ask yourself if you know the topics covered in the table.

contd

| Database Design and Development | |
|---|---|
| Analysis | Identify the end user and functional requirements of a database problem |
| Data Protection Act 1998 | Prior consent of data subject     Data used for limited, specifically stated purposes<br>Accuracy of data     Data kept safe and secure |
| Design | Entity relationship diagram for 1-to-many relationships<br>Data dictionary: tables, fields, primary key and foreign key, data types, validation<br>Query design: multiple tables, fields, search criteria, sort order |
| Implementation | Relational databases with two linked tables<br>Referential integrity<br>SQL operations:<br>— SELECT, FROM, WHERE     — UPDATE<br>— AND, OR, <, >, =     — DELETE<br>— ORDER on one or two fields     — equi-join between tables<br>— INSERT |
| Testing | SQL operations work correctly |
| Evaluation | Fitness for purpose<br>Accuracy of output |

| Web Design and Development | |
|---|---|
| Analysis | Identify the end user and functional requirements of a website |
| Website structure | Home page and up to four linked multimedia pages |
| User interface design | Visual layout and readability using a wireframe     Positioning of the media elements<br>Navigational links     File formats of the media (text, graphics,<br>Consistency across multiple pages     video, audio) |
| Copyright, Designs and Patents Act 1988 | Web content (text, graphics, video, audio) |
| Standard file formats | Audio (WAV and MP3): compression, quality, file size<br>Bit-mapped graphics (JPEG, GIF, PNG): compression, animation, transparency, colour depth |
| Factors affecting file size | Resolution, colour depth, sampling rate     The need for compression |
| Prototyping | Low fidelity using wireframe |
| Cascading Style Sheets | Internal and external     Selectors, classes and IDs<br>Properties text: font (family, size), colour, alignment, background colour |
| HTML | Tags: head, title, body, heading, paragraph, div, link, anchor, image, audio, video, lists – ol, ul and li<br>Hyperlinks (internal and external)     Relative and absolute addressing |
| JavaScript | Mouse events: onmouseover, onmouseout |
| Testing | Matches user-interface design     Media (text, graphics, video) display correctly<br>Links and navigation work correctly     Consistency |
| Evaluation | Fitness for purpose |

## Grades

You will be given an overall grade (A–D) calculated from the total of the two marks.
Typically:

- Grade A is awarded for a total of 70 per cent or more.

- Grade B is awarded for a total between 60 and 69 per cent.

- Grade C is awarded for a total between 50 and 59 per cent.

- Grade D is awarded for a total between 45 and 49 per cent.

Boundaries can vary slightly depending on the difficulty of the course assessment.

 **THINGS TO DO AND THINK ABOUT**

Don't spend too much time on a component that is not worth many marks at the
expense of losing lots of marks in a more important component.

# SOFTWARE DESIGN AND DEVELOPMENT

# ANALYSIS AND DESIGN

## INTRODUCTION

The development of software follows a series of stages in the order shown below:

1. Analysis, 2. Design, 3. Implementation, 4. Testing, 5. Evaluation.

Each stage must be completed before the next stage can begin. For example, it is not possible to design the solution to a problem until an analysis has been carried out to find out what the software is required to do.

An outline of each stage is given below.

1. **Analysis:** an investigation to determine the functional requirements of the software in terms of the inputs, processes and outputs that are to be carried out.

2. **Design:** the variables and data types required to solve the problem are identified. The structure of the program is designed as well as the detailed logic of the program code. A sketch of the user interface is created showing any inputs and outputs.

3. **Implementation:** a programming language is used to convert the design into an actual program.

4. **Testing:** the program solution is tested with carefully chosen test data to find and remove any errors.

5. **Evaluation:** the solution is assessed to determine if it is fit for purpose, efficient, robust and readable.

## ANALYSIS

Software cannot be written before a full and detailed description is identified of what it has to do. All software projects begin with a meeting with the clients to determine their needs and the functional requirements of the software.

All computer programs follow the same basic principle of inputting data, carrying out some processing of the data and then outputting the results.

Before software can be designed, it is important to clarify the functional requirements of the software in terms of its inputs, processes and outputs.

### EXAMPLE:

A program enters the names and exam marks of each of 20 students in a class. It then calculates the average mark and the student with the best mark who will get a prize, and displays the average mark and the prizewinner.
(The exam marks are entered and validated in the range 0 to 100.)

| | |
|---|---|
| Input | Enter the name and a valid mark for each of the 20 students. |
| Processing | Find the name of the prizewinner. Calculate the average of the marks. |
| Output | Display the name of the prizewinner and the average mark. |

## DESIGN

Before a piece of software is written, it goes through the process of design. The design will include a plan of the structure of the program as well as the detailed logic of the program code. It is a mistake to think that design is not necessary and that it would save time to go straight to writing the program code. This approach might be possible for a small-scale program such as a program that finds the average of three numbers. However, in a large commercial project, the design is essential to allow the allocation of sections of code to a team of programmers and to ensure that the program modules work together correctly.

Structure charts and flowcharts are used to illustrate a visual design of the program. Pseudocode is using text for designing the detailed logic of the program.

# STRUCTURE DIAGRAMS

It is much easier for a human being to solve a series of small problems than one large, complex problem. A **structure diagram** is used to split a program up into smaller, more manageable parts. This is performed in a series of steps called **stepwise refinement** in which a large problem is broken down into parts and then those parts themselves are further broken down into smaller parts. This process is repeated until the parts are small enough to be easy to solve.

A different symbol is used in a structure diagram to make it clear whether sequencing, selection or repetition is taking place.

The different symbols are given below:

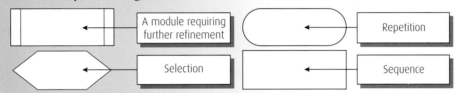

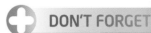

## Sequence

Sequencing is where a list of instructions is carried out one after another.

The structure diagram alongside shows the sequence of steps required for a program which calculates and displays the area of a rectangle.

The following pseudocode gives the steps required to solve the problem.

## Selection

Selection is where different sets of instructions are carried out depending upon whether a condition is true or false.

The structure diagram alongside shows the steps required for a program which enters the name of a student and an exam mark and gives a message stating whether the mark is a pass or a fail.

The following pseudocode gives the steps required to solve the same problem.

## Repetition (sometimes called iteration)

Iteration is where groups of instructions are repeated.

The structure diagram alongside shows the steps required for a program which calculates the number of passes and fails in a list of 20 exam marks.

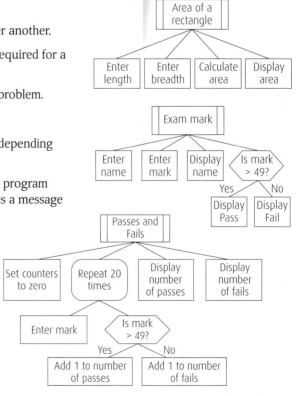

# THINGS TO DO AND THINK ABOUT

You can expect to get questions on structure diagrams in the exam – but they can also be used as a means of designing your program in the practical assignment task. If you decide to use a structure diagram in your assignment report, then make sure that you use the correct symbols.

# MORE DESIGN

## PSEUDOCODE

**Pseudocode** is used at the design stage to represent the detailed logic of the program code. It gives the same detail as the programming code but uses natural language. This allows the logic of the steps required to solve a problem to be produced without worrying about the command words and formatting required of a particular programming language.

Pseudocode shows the design of the programming constructs of sequence, selection and iteration.

## DESIGN OF PROGRAMMING CONSTRUCTS

The following examples provide pseudocode designs of sequence, selection and repetition constructs.

### Sequence

A program enters the length and breadth of a rectangle and calculates and displays the area of the rectangle.

The following pseudocode gives the steps required to solve the same problem.

```
1   RECEIVE Length FROM KEYBOARD
2   RECEIVE Breadth FROM KEYBOARD
3   SET Area TO Length * Breadth
4   SEND ["The area is: ", Area] TO DISPLAY
```

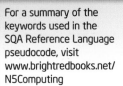

**ONLINE**

For a summary of the keywords used in the SQA Reference Language pseudocode, visit www.brightredbooks.net/ N5Computing

### Selection

A program enters the name of a student and an exam mark, then gives a message stating if the mark is a pass or a fail.

The following pseudocode gives the steps required to solve the problem. Notice that the IF ... ELSE ... END IF construct is indented to make the code stand out and be easier to read.

```
1   RECEIVE Name FROM KEYBOARD
2   RECEIVE Mark FROM KEYBOARD
3   SEND [Name] TO DISPLAY
4   IF Mark > 49 THEN
5        SEND ["Pass"] TO DISPLAY
6   ELSE
7        SEND ["Fail"] TO DISPLAY
8   END IF
```

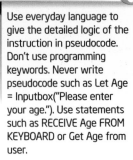

**DON'T FORGET**

Use everyday language to give the detailed logic of the instruction in pseudocode. Don't use programming keywords. Never write pseudocode such as Let Age = Inputbox("Please enter your age."). Use statements such as RECEIVE Age FROM KEYBOARD or Get Age from user.

### Iteration

A program enters 20 exam marks and calculates and displays the number of passes and fails.

The pseudocode required to solve this problem is shown below.

Notice that the FOR... END FOR construct is indented to make the code stand out and be easier to read.

```
1   SET Passes TO 0
2   SET Fails TO 0
3   FOR Count FROM 1 TO 20 DO
4        RECEIVE Mark FROM KEYBOARD
5        IF Mark > 49 THEN
6            SET Passes TO Passes + 1
7        ELSE
8            SET Fails TO Fails + 1
9        END IF
10  END FOR
11  SEND ["The number of passes is: ", Passes]
    TO DISPLAY
12  SEND ["The number of fails is: ", Fails]
    TO DISPLAY
```

contd

The following pseudocode displays the numbers in a list of 12 numbers that are under 10.

```
1  SET NumberList TO [12, 3, 8, 16, 24, 4, 17, 5, 11, 6, 15, 18]
2  FOR Index FROM 0 TO 11 DO
3      IF NumberList(Index) < 10 THEN
4          SEND [NumberList(Index)] TO DISPLAY
5      END IF
6  END FOR
```

# FLOWCHARTS

Flowcharts are used to give a graphical illustration of the sequence of steps required to solve a problem.

The steps are shown in rectangles, but diamond shapes are used to illustrate that decisions are being made. The flow around the steps is indicated with arrows.

### EXAMPLE:

Part of a "Happy Families" program enters the age of two children in a family.
(Both of the ages are validated to be less than 18 years old.)
A message is then displayed stating if the children are twins or not.
(The flowchart assumes that only twin children would have the same age.)

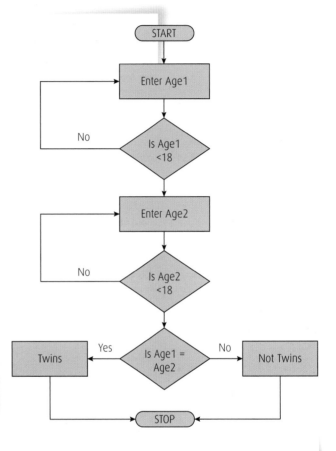

**ONLINE TEST**

Test your knowledge of design online at www.brightredbooks.net/N5Computing

 **THINGS TO DO AND THINK ABOUT**

Structure diagrams and pseudocode can both be used to illustrate the design of a program. There is not only one correct answer to the design of a program, but it is essential that your design shows all of the essential steps and any selection or iteration that is required. Illustrate the design of a program that you have written recently, both in a structure diagram and with pseudocode.

# DATA TYPES AND STRUCTURES

## VARIABLES

**Variables** are used in programs to store items of data such as a surname, age, exam mark etc. that are entered by the user or produced as the result of a calculation.

A variable is a label given to an item of data so that program instructions can work with them. It is easier to understand programs that use meaningful names for variables, such as Surname, Age and ExamMark and not S, A and E, or – even worse – X, Y and Z.

Most programming languages require the variables used in a program to be declared before they are used.

This makes the program easier to understand by clearly stating which variables are used by the program, and also allows the program to set memory aside to store the variables. In a large commercial program, the amount of data stored in variables can be several megabytes.

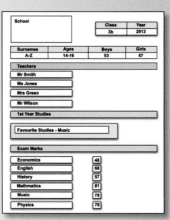

**DON'T FORGET**

The name given to a variable must not contain any spaces or start with a number. For example, ExamMark is OK but Exam Mark or 1Mark are not allowed.

**ONLINE**

Check out the tutorial about variables and data types: www.brightredbooks.net/N5Computing

## DATA TYPES

A variable such as Surname will hold a piece of text, whereas a variable called Age will hold a number. For this reason, different **data types** are needed to store different kinds of data in programs.

### Char

The Char data type is used for a variable that is storing one character.

> **EXAMPLE:**
> "T", "n", "3", "£" and so on.

### String

The **STRING** data type is used for a variable that is storing an item of text.

> **EXAMPLE:**
> "Violin", "Himalayas", Yes", "Don't walk", "F" and so on.

A STRING data type could be used in a program to store a surname, town, colour and so on.

### Integers

The **INTEGER** data type is used for a variable that is storing a positive or negative whole number.

> **EXAMPLE:**
> 18, –40, 66, 0, –555, 65,536 and so on.

An INTEGER data type could be used in a program to store an age, the number of people on a bus, the number of a ball in the National Lottery and so on.

### Real

The **REAL** data type is used for a variable that is storing a positive or negative decimal number.

**DON'T FORGET**

Schools in Scotland use different languages to teach programming. However, in the exam for this course, the questions on programming code will all be set in a language called the SQA Reference Language. This book will use the SQA Reference Language to explain programming concepts.

**contd**

> **EXAMPLE:**
>
> 2·5, 3·14, –5·77, 0, 598·67, 0·00703 and so on.

A REAL data type could be used in a program to store a height, time for a 100m race, weight and so on.

## Boolean

The **BOOLEAN** variable is a two-state variable. It can store either TRUE or FALSE.

> **EXAMPLE:**
>
> TRUE, FALSE.

A BOOLEAN data type could be used in a program to store an answer to a true-or-false quiz, whether a search item has been found or not, whether an exam mark is a pass or fail, and so on.

## Dim

Most programming languages use a DIM (dimension) statement to declare variables.

> **EXAMPLE:**
>
> DIM Age As INTEGER          DIM Found As BOOLEAN
> DIM Height As REAL          DIM Answer As CHAR
> DIM Surname As STRING

**DON'T FORGET**

When variables are declared, the name and the data type of each variable is stated.

# DATA STRUCTURES

An **array** is an example of a data structure. It is used to store a list of items which are each of the same data type: for example, a list of the names of 20 students in a class, the salary of each employee in a bank, the names of the countries at the Olympics and so on.

Each element of the array can be identified by an index number.

The example below shows a numeric array called Burgers() which is storing a list of six types of burger in a fast-food restaurant.

An index from 0 to 5 is used to identify each element.

| Burgers(0) | Burgers(1) | Burgers(2) | Burgers(3) | Burgers(4) | Burgers(5) |
|------------|------------|------------|------------|------------|------------|
| Regular | Cheese | Chicken | Double | Mega | Veggie |

Arrays must be declared at the start of a program before they can be used. The number inside the brackets specifies how many items the array can store. The data type is stated as String, Integer, Single or Boolean.

Most programming languages use a DIM statement to declare arrays.

DIM stands for dimension.

Examples of arrays of different data types:

> **EXAMPLE:**
>
> DIM Colours(9) As STRING         DIM Answers(39) As BOOLEAN
> DIM Marks(19) As INTEGER         DIM Sex(15) As CHAR
> DIM Heights(99) As REAL

**DON'T FORGET**

An array which is declared as Ages(79) as Integer can store 80 ages and not 79 ages. This is because the array includes an index of 0, so that Ages(0) holds an item of data.

**ONLINE TEST**

How well do you know data types and structures? Test yourself online at www.brightredbooks.net/N5Computing

## THINGS TO DO AND THINK ABOUT

For the main programming language that you use in your school, write down four examples of data types that the language supports. For each data type, use the program's online help to write down the range of values that the data type can be used to represent.

# PROGRAMMING CONSTRUCTS 1

## INTRODUCTION

Programs are made up of a set of instructions that are executed to solve a problem. The instructions in a program are not simply executed in order from the first instruction to the last instruction. Programs often repeat instructions to improve their efficiency or make decisions by branching to different groups of instructions depending on the value of variables.

## ASSIGNMENT

Variables are used in programs to store items of data. **Assignment** is a term used to describe the process of assigning a value to a variable.

The value assigned to the variable can be either a constant value or the result of a calculation.

### EXAMPLES:

The following expression assigns the constant value 20 to the Discount variable.

SET Discount TO 20

The following expression calculates the area of a circle from the radius and assigns it to the Area variable.

SET Area TO 3·14 * Radius ^ 2

## ARITHMETIC OPERATIONS (+, −, *, /, ^)

Programming languages perform addition, subtraction, multiplication, division and powers operations. These operations are represented by the symbols shown in the table shown alongside.

| Operation | Symbol |
|-----------|--------|
| Add | + |
| Subtract | − |
| Multiply | * |
| Divide | / |
| Power | ^ |

The following examples illustrate some uses of these operations:

### EXAMPLES:

This instruction calculates the number of pupils in a class.

SET ClassSize TO Boys + Girls

This instruction calculates an employee's net pay after tax is paid.

SET NetPay TO Hours * PayPerHour - Tax

This instruction calculates the share of the jackpot that the winners of the National Lottery receive.

SET Share TO Jackpot / NumberofWinners

This instruction calculates the area of a circle from the radius.

SET Area TO 3·14 * Radius ^ 2

### Concatenation

Concatenation is joining string variables together to make longer strings. The ampersand symbol (&) is commonly used to concatenate strings together.

The following example assigns the string "MacDonald" to the surname variable.

    Surname = "Mac" & "Donald"

The following example assigns the string "Dr. John Hemmings" to the FullName variable.

    Title = "Dr. "
    Name = "John Hemmings"
    FullName =Title & Name

## DON'T FORGET

The symbols '*' and '/' are used in programs to perform multiplication and division respectively.

## ONLINE

Check out the online calculator which works out the area of a circle from the radius: www.brightredbooks. net/N5Computing. Can you find another example of an arithmetic operation online?

## COMPARISONS

Programming languages use comparisons such as 'equal to', 'greater than' and so on.

These are represented by the symbols shown in the table alongside.

The following examples illustrate some uses of these operations:

| Comparison | Symbol |
|---|---|
| Equal to | = |
| Not equal to | <> |
| Greater than | > |
| Greater than or equal to | >= |
| Less than | < |
| Less than or equal to | <= |

### EXAMPLES:

This instruction illustrates the 'equal to' comparison.
IF Age = 5 THEN SEND ["You are old enough to start school."] TO DISPLAY

This instruction illustrates the 'not equal to' comparison.
IF Age <> 0 THEN SEND ["You have had at least one birthday."] TO DISPLAY

This instruction illustrates the 'greater than' comparison.
IF Age > 65 THEN SEND ["You should be retired."] TO DISPLAY

This instruction illustrates the 'greater than or equal to' comparison.
IF Age >= 40 THEN SEND ["Life begins at forty."] TO DISPLAY

This instruction illustrates the 'less than' comparison.
IF Age < 18 THEN SEND ["You are a child."] TO DISPLAY

This instruction illustrates the 'less than or equal to' comparison.
IF Age <= 99 THEN SEND ["You are not a century old yet."] TO DISPLAY

 **DON'T FORGET**

It is more efficient to use the 'power' symbol than to multiply a variable by itself. For example, Length ^ 3 is more efficient than Length * Length * Length.

## SEQUENCE

**Sequencing** is when the program executes a list of instructions one after another.

The following program is an example of sequencing. It enters the sides of a cuboid and then calculates and displays the volume of the cuboid. The instructions in this program are executed in sequence one after the other. There is no repetition of instructions or branching within the program.

```
RECEIVE Length FROM KEYBOARD
RECEIVE Breadth FROM KEYBOARD
RECEIVE Height FROM KEYBOARD
SET Volume TO Length * Breadth * Height
SEND ["The volume of the cuboid is: ", Volume] TO DISPLAY
```

This program is an example of Input-Process-Output, where a program enters data, performs a calculation and then displays the result of the calculation. This is essentially how all programs work.

 **DON'T FORGET**

The 'greater than or equal to' and the 'less than or equal' to comparisons require two symbols because a keyboard does not have one key to represent this comparison.

 THINGS TO DO AND THINK ABOUT

Each programming language has different ways of writing the program instructions. Both of the following instructions do the same thing, i.e. they calculate the area of a rectangle. Let Area = Length * Breadth, Let Area := Length * Breadth. Can you think of another two sets of instructions to calculate the area of a circle?

 **ONLINE TEST**

Test your knowledge of programming constructs online at www.brightredbooks.net/N5Computing

# PROGRAMMING CONSTRUCTS 2

## SELECTION

Computer programs require to make decisions and execute different sets of instructions depending on the value of variables. For example, a program will take a different action if an exam mark is a pass than if the mark is a fail. The term **selection** describes the process of branching in a program by selecting different sets of instructions to meet the processing demands of different cases.

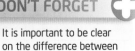

**DON'T FORGET**

It is a common mistake to mix up the comparison < with <=. The statement Age < 18 is false when Age is storing the number 18, but the statement Age <= 18 would be true. This is because 18 is not less than 18! The same principle applies to conditions using the comparisons > and >=.

## CONDITIONAL STATEMENTS

A **conditional statement** is a statement that is either true or false.

For example, the statement Age < 18 can be either true or false depending upon the value of the variable Age. If Age is storing the number 13, then the statement is true (since 13 is less than 18), but if Age is storing the number 21 then the statement is false (since 21 is not less than 18).

### Simple condition

A simple condition depends upon one conditional statement being true or false.

Programming languages use the IF ... THEN ... ELSE ... END IF construct to execute one set of instructions if a condition is true and another set of instructions if a condition is false. The ELSE part is optional, since sometimes a program requires to perform an action if a condition is true but to do nothing if the condition is false.

This conditional statement illustrates an IF statement without an ELSE.

```
IF Month = 6 THEN SEND ["The month is June."] TO DISPLAY
```

This conditional statement illustrates an IF statement with an ELSE.

```
IF Speed > 30 THEN
    SEND ["Too fast! Slow down."] TO DISPLAY
ELSE
    SEND ["Well done. Nice speed."] TO DISPLAY
END IF
```

### Complex condition

**DON'T FORGET**

It is important to be clear on the difference between the AND and OR logical operators. An AND logical operator means that both of the conditions must be true. An OR operator means that just one of the conditions must be true.

A complex condition depends upon two or more conditional statements being true or false. Programming languages have logical operators (AND, OR, NOT etc.) that can be used to implement complex conditions in program instructions.

### AND

The AND logical operator requires both conditions to be true.

The following IF statement is true only if both of the conditions Sex = "M" AND Age < 18 are true.

```
IF Sex = "M" AND Age < 18 THEN SEND ["You are a boy."] TO DISPLAY
```

contd

**ONLINE**

As well as the OR logical operator, there is an EOR logical operator. Use a search engine to investigate the difference between these two operators.

## OR

The OR logical operator requires one of the conditions to be true.

The following IF statement is true if either Day = "Sat" is true OR Day = "Sun" is true.

```
IF Day = "Sat" OR Day = "Sun" THEN SEND ["It's the weekend!"] TO DISPLAY
```

## NOT

The NOT logical operator switches a statement that is false to a statement that is true and vice versa. In other words, if a statement is not false then it is true, or if it is not true then it is false.

The following IF statement is true if Temperature > 0 is false.

```
IF NOT (Temperature > 0) THEN SEND ["It's freezing!"] TO DISPLAY
```

## SELECT CASE

Sometimes, when a program requires many IF statements to cover many selections, it is better to use a SELECT CASE construct. This construct allows different instructions to be selected depending on the value of a variable and is more readable than the alternative, which would be using lots of IF statements.

The following example illustrates the use of a SELECT ... CASE ... END SELECT to display an exam grade depending on a percentage mark.

```
SELECT CASE Percentage
CASE 0 To 49
    SEND ["Too bad. You failed!"] TO DISPLAY
CASE 50 To 59
    SEND ["You gained a C pass!"] TO DISPLAY
CASE 60 To 69
    SEND ["You gained a B pass!"] TO DISPLAY
CASE 70 To 100
    SEND ["You gained an A pass!"] TO DISPLAY
END SELECT
```

**ONLINE TEST**

Test your knowledge of programming constructs online at www.brightredbooks.net/N5Computing

## THINGS TO DO AND THINK ABOUT

Sequencing is when programs execute one instruction after another. However, programs will often use selection, which is when they branch to one or another set of instructions depending on what processing is required for a given situation. Selection can be implemented by using an IF ... THEN ... ELSE ... END IF or a SELECT ... CASE ... END SELECT control construct.

# PROGRAMMING CONSTRUCTS 3

## ITERATION

**Iteration** is the process where programs repeat a group of instructions two or more times. Iteration is also known as repetition and looping. Iteration makes programs more efficient by inserting the code to be repeated only once rather than having the same code inserted into the program several times.

## FIXED LOOPS

A **fixed loop** is a when a group of instructions is repeated a pre-determined number of times.

The instructions that are to be repeated are placed between the command words FOR ... FROM ... TO ... DO and END FOR. The number of times that the loop is to be repeated is determined by the FOR ... FROM ... TO ... DO command words, which set the start and end value of a loop counter. The END FOR command sets the end point of the instructions that are to be repeated.

The example alongside illustrates the use of a fixed loop to display an address used for labels 6 times. The loop counter (in this case Label_Number) goes from 1 to 6.

```
FOR Label_Number FROM 1 TO 6  DO
    SEND ["Miss S. Candy,"] TO DISPLAY
    SEND ["7 Sugar Crescent,"] TO DISPLAY
    SEND ["Rock City,"] TO DISPLAY
    SEND ["Wyoming,"] TO DISPLAY
    SEND ["U.S.A."] TO DISPLAY
END FOR
```

The example alongside illustrates the use of a fixed loop to display the squares of whole numbers from 0 to 20. The loop counter (in this case Number) goes from 0 to 20.

```
FOR Number FROM 0 TO 20 DO
    SEND [Number ^ 2] TO DISPLAY
END FOR
```

**ONLINE**

Visit www.brightredbooks.net/N5Computing and click on the 'Scratch' link to create your own looped programme.

The example alongside shows a fixed loop in the games development program Scratch. This loop is repeated 10 times to perform an animation by changing a costume every tenth of a second.

## CONDITIONAL LOOPS

A **conditional loop** is when a group of instructions is repeated until or while a condition is true. An example of a conditional loop is a REPEAT ... UNTIL ... loop. The instructions could be executed only once if the condition is true the first time through the loop, or the instructions could be repeated many times until a condition is true.

Another conditional loop is a WHILE ... DO ... END WHILE loop, which only executes the instructions in a loop while a condition is true. The instructions in the loop might not be executed at all if the condition is not true when first entering the loop.

The following example illustrates the use of a conditional loop where the user is repeatedly asked to guess a mystery number until the user guesses correctly.

**DON'T FORGET**

Input validation is another example of a conditional loop where a loop is used to repeatedly enter an item of data until it is valid. The data could be valid the first time that it is entered, or it could take many repeated attempts before it is accepted by the program.

```
REPEAT
    RECEIVE Guess FROM KEYBOARD
    IF Guess <> MysteryNumber THEN SEND ["Wrong. Try again!"] TO DISPLAY
UNTIL Guess = MysteryNumber
```

This code could be executed once if the user guesses correctly on the first attempt, but it could be executed many times until the user guesses correctly.

contd

The example alongside shows a conditional loop in the games development program Scratch. A superhero is given three lives, but if he/she touches a baddie then the number of lives is reduced by one. The number of times that the loop is repeated is not fixed but will continue until the number of lives falls to zero.

### Nested Loops

A **nested loop** is when one loop is placed completely inside another loop. The loops can be any combination of fixed and conditional loops.

The example alongside is of a nested loop which uses a fixed loop to enter the ages of 12 students and an inner conditional loop to validate that each age is in the range 12 to 18.

```
FOR Student FROM 0 TO 11 DO
    REPEAT
        RECEIVE Age(Student) FROM KEYBOARD
        IF Age(Student) < 12 OR Age(Student) > 18 THEN
            SEND ["The age must be between 12 and 18"] TO DISPLAY
        END IF
    UNTIL Age(Student) > 11 AND Age(Student) < 19
END FOR
```

## PRE-DEFINED FUNCTIONS

A function is used in a program to return a single item of data.

A **pre-defined function** is a function already built into the programming language which performs mathematical calculations, manipulates text, formats values and so on. Pre-defined functions can save the programmer a lot of time, since a tried and tested function is available and the code does not need to be written from scratch. Most programming languages have hundreds of pre-defined functions to meet the variety of processing requirements of different application areas.

RND is a function that selects a random number between 0·000000 and 0·999999.

The following example simulates a dice throw by picking a random number between 1 and 6.

```
Throw = INT(RND * 6) + 1
```

Multiplying RND by 6 gives a number between 0·000000 and 5·999999, and then INT(RND * 6) is used to select the integer part of the number, which is the integer 0, 1, 2, 3, 4 or 5.

Adding 1 gives an integer which is 1, 2, 3, 4, 5 or 6.

ROUND is a function that returns a decimal number rounded to a specified number of decimal places.

The following example rounds the variable Height to decimal places and displays "Your height in centimetres is 149·74."

```
Height = 149·739
"Your height in centimetres is " & ROUND(Height, 2) & "· "
```

LEN is a function which returns the number of characters in a piece of text.

The following example returns the value 5.

```
LEN("Hippo")
```

**ONLINE TEST**

Test your knowledge of programming constructs online at www.brightredbooks.net/N5Computing

## THINGS TO DO AND THINK ABOUT

The programming languages that you use for your practical work will have their own means of implementing sequence, selection and iteration. The format of the instructions may be different, but they are essentially carrying out the same processing. You should think about when sequencing, selection and iteration are required in your own programs.

# STANDARD ALGORITHMS

## INTRODUCTION

Many algorithms are used in programs over and over again. These are called **standard algorithms** or common algorithms. For example, finding the maximum value could be used in a program to find the highest exam mark in a group of students, the longest jump in a long-jump competition, the hottest day in a month of temperatures, and so on. All of these examples are using the same algorithm, and it is important to know standard algorithms so that you can implement them in your own programs.

Most programmers will have a module library of pre-written standard algorithms so that these can be inserted into the program without the need to write the code from scratch.

**ONLINE**

For more information on input validation, visit www.brightredbooks.net/N5Computing

**DON'T FORGET**

You should learn this pseudocode as a template solution for input validation. All that needs to change for different input validations is the name of the variable and the values between which it must lie. For example, validating that a month is in the range 1 to 12 would still require the same 6 lines of logic. However, the Percentage variable would be replaced with Month. The numbers 0 and 100 would be replaced with 1 and 12 in line 3, and the numbers –1 and 101 would be replaced with 0 and 13 in line 6.

## INPUT VALIDATION

Most programs require the user to enter data from the keyboard. It is very easy for the user to make a mistake and enter data that is not possible. **Input validation** is where the program repeatedly asks for an item of data to be entered until it is within the possible range of values. For example, a month is entered until it is in the range 1 to 12.

When data is entered that is not possible, an error message should give the user feedback on their mistake.

The input-validation algorithm is an example of a conditional loop.

Shown below is pseudocode for an input-validation algorithm.

```
1   REPEAT
2       RECEIVE Value FROM KEYBOARD
3       IF Value is not in range THEN
4           SEND ["Not possible. Try again!"] TO DISPLAY
5       END IF
6   UNTIL Value is in range
```

The particular example of input validation shown below enters and validates a percentage mark so that it is in the range 0 to 100.

```
1   REPEAT
2   RECEIVE Percentage FROM KEYBOARD
3       IF Percentage < 0 OR Percentage > 100 THEN
4           SEND ["Not possible. Try again!"] TO DISPLAY
5       END IF
6   UNTIL Percentage > –1 AND Percentage < 101
```

**ONLINE TEST**

Test your knowledge of standard algorithms online at www.brightredbooks.net/N5Computing

Apart from data being validated to be in a certain range of values, it can also be validated to be a certain length. For example, a date of birth can be validated to only be accepted if it is 6 digits long: 120656 and so on. Data can also be validated to be of a certain type. For example, a number must be entered and not a letter.

# RUNNING TOTAL

A lot of programs need to calculate a running total to find the sum of a list of numbers or to calculate an average.

Values are repeatedly input in a loop and are added to a running total each time round the loop.

The average can be found by dividing the final total by the number of items.

This example enters and adds up 6 numbers and displays the total and the average.

The numbers are stored in an array called List()

```
1   SET Total TO 0
2   FOR Count FROM 0 TO 5 DO
3         RECEIVE List(Count) FROM KEYBOARD
4         SET Total TO Total + List(Count)
5   END FOR
6   SEND ["The total is ", Total] TO DISPLAY
7   SET Average TO Total / 6
8   SEND ["The average is ", Average] TO DISPLAY
```

# TRAVERSING A 1-D ARRAY

A lot of programs need to pass through each element of an array in turn, from the first element to the last element while performing some processing on each element.

The example below traverses an array of 8 elements and outputs the values that are under 10·0.

```
1   SET List TO [11·23, 10·64, 9·87, 10·18, 11·67, 11·03, 9·93, 11·52]
2   FOR Count FROM 0 TO 7 DO
3         IF List(Count) < 10 THEN
4               SEND [List(Count)] TO DISPLAY
5         END IF
6   END FOR

Output
9·87
9·93
```

## DON'T FORGET

The first index in an array is 0 and not 1. To traverse an array of 20 elements, the index should loop from 0 to 19 and not 1 to 20.

## ONLINE

There are other standard algorithms apart from the ones listed here. Enter the keywords 'standard algorithm' and 'pseudocode' into a search engine to investigate further examples and what they are used for. For example, a maximum value and a linear search are commonly used in programs.

## THINGS TO DO AND THINK ABOUT

You are expected to know the pseudocode for the input-validation algorithm, and you should also be able to implement this algorithm in your programs.

Write down three examples of data that can be validated to lie within a certain range of values, and give the range of values.

# TESTING

## INTRODUCTION

The purpose of testing is to detect and remove errors in a program. Programs should be comprehensively tested to see whether they give the correct results when dealing with normal everyday data, extreme data which lies on the boundaries, and exceptional data which is outwith the expected limits.

## ERRORS

Errors are classified into three different types: syntax, execution and logic errors.

### Syntax errors

**Syntax errors** are identified and reported by the translator program when the program is translated.

Syntax errors can take the form of misspelt command words, missing brackets, misplaced commas and so on.

Shown below are some examples of syntax errors in the Visual Basic programming language.

Misspelt language keywords          Inpot, Nxt I, Repeet
Missing brackets                    Let Score = InputBox("Enter your score."
Missing inverted commas             Let Colour = "Scarlet.

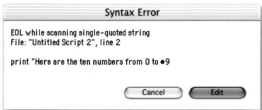

### Execution errors

**Execution errors** are errors that are detected during the running of the program.

A common execution error is to divide by zero, which is not mathematically possible and causes an error.

### Logic errors

Sometimes, a program can run to completion without crashing or any sign of a problem. However, it could be that there are mistakes in the code that cause errors in the calculations, and the program does not produce the correct results.

These are errors in the logic of the code itself: for example, writing code to add two numbers instead of multiplying them, or subtracting two numbers the wrong way round.

Shown below is an example of a **logical error**.

```
'Find the range of scores from highest to lowest
Let Range = MinScore - MaxScore
```

This instruction is supposed to find the range of values between a highest and a lowest score. By subtracting the highest score from the lowest score, it gives an error, since it should be subtracting the lowest score from the highest score.

**DON'T FORGET**

Execution errors are sometimes called runtime errors. Both these terms mean the same thing.

**ONLINE**

For more on programming errors, visit www.brightredbooks.net/N5Computing

## NORMAL, EXTREME AND EXCEPTIONAL TEST DATA

Programs are not tested in a makeshift, random fashion. A program should be tested methodically with **normal data**, **extreme data** and then **exceptional data** to make sure that it gives correct results when dealing with as many scenarios as possible.

contd

## Normal

One set of test data should be chosen to test that the software gives correct results for everyday data which is within the expected range of values.

For example, if a program is entering a percentage mark, then normal data could be 72 and 45.

## Extreme

One set of test data should be chosen to see whether the software can handle data which lies on the boundaries of possible data.

For example, if a program is entering a percentage mark, then extreme data could be 0 and 100.

## Exceptional

One set of test data should be chosen for unusual cases to test whether the software can deal with unexpected data without crashing.

For example, if a program is entering a percentage mark, then exceptional data could be 199, –40, Yes, G12 and so on.

**DON'T FORGET**

Sometimes, extreme data is referred to as boundary data. Both of these terms mean the same thing, which is test data that is on the limits of normal data.

**ONLINE**

What percentage of the time in software development do you think is spent on testing? Use a search engine to get an estimate of the percentage time, using keywords such as 'software development', 'testing', 'percentage' and so on. You might be surprised by the answer.

## EXAMPLES OF TESTING

A program prompts the user to enter the exam marks of 6 students as a percentage. The program then displays the number of students who achieved each of the following grades. (A grade is 70 to 100, B grade is 60 to 69, C grade is 50 to 59, Fail is 0 to 49.)

The program also validates that the entered marks are in the range 0 to 100.

Shown below is an example of how to test a program by first choosing the test data with reasons for your choice and then working out the expected results on paper. The test data can then be entered into the program on the computer to see whether it gives the same results as those that have been manually calculated.

The following are examples of normal, extreme and exceptional test data that could be used to test this program. A reason is given for choosing each set of test data, together with the expected results.

| | |
|---|---|
| **Normal** test data | 56, 32, 66, 89, 62, 43 |
| Reason for choice | This data has been chosen to see whether the program gives correct results for everyday marks that give a mixture of A, B and C grades and fails. |
| Expected results | A grades 1, B grades 2, C grades 1, Fails 2 |
| **Extreme** test data | 60, 0, 70, 100, 49, 50 |
| Reason for choice | This data has been chosen to see whether the program gives correct results for marks that lie on the boundaries of the grades. |
| Expected results | A grades 2, B grades 1, C grades 1, Fails 2 |
| **Exceptional** test data | 199, –66, X, £, 7?, cat |
| Reason for choice | This data has been chosen to see whether the program gives correct results for marks that are not valid percentage exam marks. |
| Expected results | The program should give an error message and ask for valid marks to be entered. |

**ONLINE TEST**

For a testing test (on testing), go to www.brightredbooks.net/N5Computing

**DON'T FORGET**

When testing your own programs, it is important to give a reason for choosing your test data and not just the test data itself. You should also work out on paper the expected results that the program should give with the test data. This is called a dry run.

## THINGS TO DO AND THINK ABOUT

Testing program code is not just a topic for the theory questions in the exam. You must also make sure that you comprehensively test your own programs in your practical work by supplying normal, extreme and exceptional test data.

# EVALUATION

## FIT FOR PURPOSE

Once a software project has been completed, it should be evaluated to assess whether or not it solves the problem that it is supposed to solve.

Software is said to be fit for purpose if it fulfils the requirements which were identified at the analysis stage.

## EFFICIENT CODE

A program is efficient if the length of its code or speed of execution is proportional to the scale of the program.

### Use of loops

The use of repetition can improve the efficiency by repeating instructions in a loop rather than using a sequence of individual instructions.

| Program 1 |
|---|
| 1    SEND [1 ^ 2] TO DISPLAY |
| 2    SEND [2 ^ 2] TO DISPLAY |
| 3    SEND [3 ^ 2] TO DISPLAY |
| 4    SEND [4 ^ 2] TO DISPLAY |
| 5    SEND [5 ^ 2] TO DISPLAY |
| 6    SEND [6 ^ 2] TO DISPLAY |
| 7    SEND [7 ^ 2] TO DISPLAY |
| 8    SEND [8 ^ 2] TO DISPLAY |
| 9    SEND [9 ^ 2] TO DISPLAY |
| 10   SEND [10 ^ 2] TO DISPLAY |

**EXAMPLE:**

Both of the programs shown display the squares of the numbers from 1 up to 10.
Program 1 uses a sequence of 10 instructions to solve the problem.
Program 2 is a more efficient use of code since it uses a loop to repeat the same instruction 10 times.

### Arrays

Using arrays for a list of related data is much more efficient than using separate variables. Using an array allows the elements to be processed in a loop rather than having repeated code to process each separate variable.

### Nested IFs

Using nested IFs instead of multiple IFs produces more efficient code since less execution of instructions is required.

| Program 2 |
|---|
| 1    FOR Number FROM 1 TO 10 DO |
| 2       SEND [Number ^ 2] TO DISPLAY |
| 3    END FOR |

**EXAMPLE:**

Both of the programs below display the result of a football match from the number of goals scored by Team A and Team B.

Program 1 uses multiple IFs, which is inefficient, since if the first IF is true then the remaining IFs are still executed to see if they are true even though they could not be true.

Program 2 uses nested IFs, which is more efficient, since if the first IF is true then the rest of the code is not executed because it is part of the ELSE.

| Program 1 |
|---|
| IF GoalsA = GoalsB THEN |
|     SEND ["Draw"] TO DISPLAY |
| |
| END IF |
| IF GoalsA > GoalsB THEN |
|     SEND ["Team A won"] TO DISPLAY |
| |
| END IF |
| IF GoalsA < GoalsB THEN |
|     SEND ["Team B won"] TO DISPLAY |
| |
| END IF |

| Program 2 |
|---|
| IF GoalsA = GoalsB THEN |
|     SEND ["Draw"] TO DISPLAY |
| ELSE |
|     IF GoalsA > GoalsB THEN |
|         SEND ["Team A won"] TO DISPLAY |
|     ELSE |
|         SEND ["Team B won"] TO DISPLAY |
|     END IF |
| END IF |

# ROBUSTNESS

A program is robust if it can cope with unexpected input or mishaps without crashing.

For example, if a program is expecting a number to be entered and the user enters a piece of text, then the program should give an error message and request the user to re-enter the number, and should not simply crash.

# READABILITY

A **readable** program is a program that is easily understood by another programmer.

Programs are made readable by using techniques that include inserting internal commentary, or using meaningful variable names and indentations.

It is important that programs are readable so that they can be easily understood and updated in the future.

## Internal commentary

Programming languages allow the programmer to insert comments to explain what the instructions are doing. This is known as **internal commentary**. The comments are not executed when the program is executed but are only there to help a programmer make sense of the program code.

## Meaningful identifiers

Variable names are the labels a programmer gives for items of data used by the program. It is important to choose **meaningful identifiers** that relate to the data in a meaningful way. Variable names such as BestScore and WorstScore make it much easier to understand the program code than variable names such as B and W.

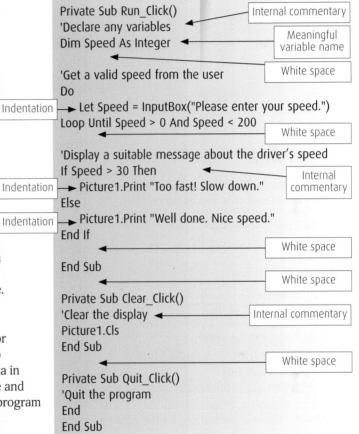

```
Private Sub Run_Click()        Internal commentary
'Declare any variables
Dim Speed As Integer           Meaningful variable name

                               White space
'Get a valid speed from the user
Do
   Let Speed = InputBox("Please enter your speed.")   Indentation
Loop Until Speed > 0 And Speed < 200
                               White space
'Display a suitable message about the driver's speed
If Speed > 30 Then             Internal commentary
   Picture1.Print "Too fast! Slow down."   Indentation
Else
   Picture1.Print "Well done. Nice speed."   Indentation
End If
                               White space
End Sub
                               White space
Private Sub Clear_Click()
'Clear the display            Internal commentary
Picture1.Cls
End Sub
                               White space
Private Sub Quit_Click()
'Quit the program
End
End Sub
```

## Indentation

**Indentation** makes it easier to identify the control constructs in the code, such as which sections of code are repeated and which instructions are selected for execution in an IF ... THEN ... ELSE ... END IF construct.

## White space

White space is blank areas in the program listing such as blank lines between control constructs and procedures and indentation in loops and IFs.

# THINGS TO DO AND THINK ABOUT

Different programming languages have different ways of entering internal commentary. Research how to enter internal commentary in JavaScript, HTML and Python.

# QUESTIONS AND ANSWERS 1

## QUESTION 1

The development of a star sign program proceeds through a series of stages as shown below.

**(a)** State the names of the missing **two** stages.

Analysis, _____ , Implementation, _____ , Evaluation

**(b)** The program is required to enter the name and date of birth of the user. It then displays a message stating their name, star sign and how many days that they have been alive for.

Identify all inputs, processes and outputs for this program.

Marks 2, 3

## QUESTION 2

A program enters the name, age and height of an applicant for a pilot training course. It then displays a message saying whether the candidate is successful or not.

To be successful, a candidate must be between 18 and 26 years old inclusive and less than 1·8 metres tall.

Part of the program is shown below. The program contains two errors.

```
SET Suitable TO TRUE
RECEIVE Name FROM KEYBOARD
RECEIVE Age FROM KEYBOARD
IF Age < 18 AND Age > 26 THEN SET Suitable TO FALSE
RECEIVE Height FROM KEYBOARD
IF Height < 1·8 THEN SET Suitable TO FALSE
IF Suitable = TRUE THEN
    SEND ["Welcome to the pilot training course."] TO DISPLAY
ELSE
    SEND ["You are not suitable for the pilot training course."] TO DISPLAY
END IF
```

**(a)** State a suitable data type for the variables Name, Age, Height and Suitable.

**(b)** Explain why you chose each data type.

**(c)** There is a mistake in the two instructions shown below.

IF Age < 18 AND Age > 26 THEN SET Suitable TO FALSE

IF Height < 1·8 THEN SET Suitable TO FALSE

Explain the error in each instruction, and write down the corrected instruction.

**(d)** Rewrite both of the following instructions more efficiently by using a different arithmetic operator.

**(i)** The following instruction is used to treble the score of a player in a game.

SET Score TO Score + Score + Score

**(ii)** The following instruction is used to find the volume of a cube.

SET CubeVolume TO Length * Length * Length

Marks 4, 4, 4, 1, 1

## QUESTION 3

A program stores the names of 60 zoo animals in an array. The program declares the array as shown below.

```
DIM Animals(59) As STRING
```

Show how an array could be declared to store each of the following data.

**(a)** The distances in metres for 20 athletes in a long-jump final.

contd

**(b)** The names of 10 famous people in Scotland.

**(c)** The answers to a multiple-choice quiz which has 25 True or False answers.

**(d)** The seven numbers that are drawn in a National Lottery draw.

**Marks 1, 1, 1, 1**

# QUESTION 4

In a game, a player throws two dice and wins a bonus point if a total score of more than 6 is thrown, otherwise a bonus point is deducted. Pseudocode representing part of the program code is shown alongside.

```
SET Total TO Die1 + Die2
IF Total > 6 THEN
    SET Bonus TO Bonus + 1
ELSE
    SET Bonus TO Bonus - 1
END IF
```

**(a)** The rules of the game are to be changed so that a bonus point is awarded for a total score between 8 and 11 inclusive, otherwise a bonus point is deducted.

Write down a complex condition that would update the program to work correctly for the new rules.

**(b)** A program enters a temperature and then displays a message saying whether it is freezing or not. (Freezing is zero degrees or below.)

Which of the following conditions are correct?

**A**  IF Temperature > 0 THEN SEND ["It's freezing!"] TO DISPLAY

**B**  IF NOT (Temperature > 0) THEN SEND ["It's freezing!"] TO DISPLAY

**C**  IF Temperature <= 0 THEN SEND ["It's freezing!"] TO DISPLAY

**D**  IF NOT (Temperature <= 0) SEND ["It's freezing!"] TO DISPLAY

**Marks 2, 2**

## ANSWER TO QUESTION 1

**(a)** Design and testing

**(b)** Input      Enter the name and date of birth.

Processing  Find the star sign and the number of days since the birthday.

Output      Display the name, star sign and days since the user was born.

## ANSWER TO QUESTION 2

**(a)** Name should be a STRING data type.

Age should be an INTEGER data type.

Height should be a REAL data type.

Suitable should be a BOOLEAN data type.

**(b)** The Name variable is storing a piece of text.

The Age variable is storing a whole number, such as 21, 16, 27 and so on.

The Height variable is storing a number which can be a decimal fraction, such as 1·83, 1·69 and so on.

The Suitable variable is storing either True or False.

**(c)** The condition IF Age > 18 AND Age > 26 can never be true since Age can't be both less than 18 and more than 26 at the same time. The AND should be replaced with an OR so that, if the candidate is under 18 or over 26, then he/she is not suitable.

The correct instruction should be:

IF Age < 18 OR Age > 26 THEN SET Suitable TO FALSE

The candidate is not suitable if he/she is 1·8 m tall or more

The condition IF Height < 1·8 THEN SET Suitable TO FALSE states that a Height of less than 1·8 is unsuitable.

The correct instruction should be:

IF Height >= 1·8 THEN SET Suitable TO FALSE

## ANSWER TO QUESTION 2

**(d)** (i) The addition operator should be replaced by a multiplication operator.

SET Score TO 3 * Score

(ii) The multiplication operator should be replaced by a power operator.

SET CubeVolume TO Length ^ 3

## ANSWER TO QUESTION 3

**(a)** DIM Distances(19) As REAL

**(b)** DIM People(9) As STRING

**(c)** DIM Answers(24) As BOOLEAN

**(d)** DIM Numbers(6) As INTEGER

## ANSWER TO QUESTION 4

**(a)** IF Total > 7 AND Total < 12 THEN

There are other correct answers which use the 'greater than or equal to' symbols or the 'less than or equal to' symbols.

IF Total >= 8 AND Total <= 11 THEN

IF Total > 7 AND Total <= 11 THEN

IF Total >= 8 AND Total < 12 THEN

**(b)** A  False

B  True

C  True

D  False

# QUESTIONS AND ANSWERS 2

## QUESTION 1

Sophie is writing a program that will be used to teach children simple mathematics.

Her program uses fixed and conditional loops to repeat instructions.

**(a)** Which type of loop is being used in each section of code shown below?

| Code A | Code B |
|---|---|
| FOR Number FROM 1 TO 12 DO<br>   SEND [Number * 7] TO DISPLAY<br>END FOR | SET Number TO 0<br>REPEAT<br>   SET Number TO Number + 1<br>   SEND [Number ^ 2] TO DISPLAY<br>UNTIL Number ^ 2 = 100 |

**(b)** Explain the difference between these two types of loops.

**(c)** A program enters the age of a school pupil which must be a number in the range 5 to 18. State which type of loop is used to validate the input.

**Marks 2, 2, 1**

## QUESTION 2

Harry writes computer programs for an insurance company. He uses a lot of pre-defined functions when writing his programs.

**(a)** Describe two advantages to Harry of using pre-defined functions.

**(b)** The Mid function returns a piece of text from a string variable by specifying the string, a starting position and the number of characters to select.

Study the first two examples and then write down the text returned by the third Mid function.

| | | |
|---|---|---|
| Example 1 | Mid ("Holidays", 5, 3) | Returns the text "day". |
| Example 2 | Mid ("Balance", 2, 4) | Returns the text "alan". |
| Example 3 | Mid ("Mississippi", 7, 3) | ? |

**Marks 2, 2**

## QUESTION 3

Shown alongside is a flowchart illustrating a programming algorithm.

Examine the steps and explain the purpose of the flowchart.

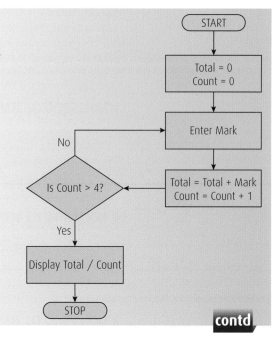

contd

**(b)** A program simulates a game of dice between two players. In a round, each player rolls two dice and accumulates a total for the points scored on the two dice. The first player to gain a lead of 13 points or more after a round is declared the winner.

Produce pseudocode to solve this problem by putting the following steps into the correct order.

| IF TotalA - TotalB > 12 THEN | SEND ["A Won!"] TO DISPLAY |

| SET ThrowB TO RANDOM 0...12 | ELSE |

UNTIL TotalA - TotalB > 12 OR TotalB - TotalA > 12

| SET TotalA TO TotalA + ThrowA | SET TotalB to 0 |

| REPEAT | END IF | SEND ["B Won!"] TO DISPLAY |

| SET ThrowA TO RANDOM 0...12 | SET TotalA to 0 |

SET TotalB TO TotalB + ThrowB

**Marks 3, 5**

## QUESTION 4

A program enters the names and heights of two sisters. The program then calculates and displays the name of the taller sister.

Illustrate a solution to this problem in a structure chart.

**Marks 4**

### ANSWER TO QUESTION 4

The following structure diagram solves the problem.

```
                          Taller Sister
   ┌──────┬────────┬───────────┬───────────┬──────────────┐
Enter     Enter    Enter       Enter       Is              
Name1     Name2    Height1     Height2     Height1 > Height2?
                                            Yes ┐   No ┐
                                          Display   Display
                                          Name1     Name2
```

### ANSWER TO QUESTION 3

**(a)** The code enters five marks while keeping a running total of the marks and then calculates and displays the average of the five marks.

**(b)** The following pseudocode solves the problem.

| 1 | SET TotalA to 0 |
| 2 | SET TotalB to 0 |
| 3 | REPEAT |
| 4 | SET ThrowA TO RANDOM 0...12 |
| 5 | SET TotalA TO TotalA + ThrowA |
| 6 | SET ThrowB TO RANDOM 0...12 |
| 7 | SET TotalB TO TotalB + ThrowB |
| 8 | UNTIL TotalA - TotalB > 12 OR TotalB - TotalA > 12 |
| 9 | IF TotalA - TotalB > 12 THEN |
| 10 | SEND ["A Won!"] TO DISPLAY |
| 11 | ELSE |
| 11 | SEND ["B Won!"] TO DISPLAY |
| 13 | END IF |

### ANSWER TO QUESTION 2

**(a)** The programmer saves time because he/she does not have to write the instructions from scratch.

Also, the function is tried and tested and will be free of errors, which might not be the case if written by the programmer.

**(b)** Mid ("Mississippi", 7, 3) returns the text "sip".

### ANSWER TO QUESTION 1

**(a)** Code A is using a fixed loop.

Code B is using a conditional loop.

**(b)** A fixed loop repeats a group of instructions a pre-determined number of times.

A conditional loop repeats a group of instructions until a condition is true.

**(c)** Validation requires a conditional loop.

# QUESTIONS AND ANSWERS 3

## QUESTION 1

Program instructions often make use of concatenation.

**(a)** Describe what is meant by the term 'concatenation'.

**(b)** Which data type does concatenation operate on?

**(c)** Which symbol is used to perform concatenation?

A program contains four string variables called Firstname, Surname, Title and Qualification.

The variables are currently storing "Molly", "Miller", "Mrs" and "B.Sc." respectively.

**(d)** Write down the string that is returned by each of the following expressions:

(i) Firstname & " " & Surname

(ii) Title & " " & Surname & " " & Qualification

**Marks 1, 1, 1, 2**

## QUESTION 2

Most high-level languages have pre-defined functions such as LEN and ROUND.

**(a)** Describe the purpose of the LEN and ROUND functions.

**(b)** Copy and complete the sentences below to give the value returned by each of the pre-defined functions.

(i) LEN("Hello")

Returns _____

(ii) LEN("Mr President")

Returns _____

(iii) LEN("Good" & " " & "boy.")

Returns _____

(iv) ROUND(34·619, 1)

Returns _____

(v) ROUND(0·087803, 2)

Returns _____

(vi) ROUND(50·3175, 3)

Returns _____

**(c)** Name two other examples of pre-defined functions.

**Marks 2,6, 2**

## QUESTION 3

Many computer games make use of a random-number function to put an element of chance into selections.

For example, games that involve dealing cards and dice-throws need to assign a random value to a variable.

**(a)** A computer program uses the following instruction:
X = Int(Rnd * 52)

(i) Explain the purpose of this instruction.

(ii) Suggest a computer game that might use this code, and justify your answer.

contd

**(b)** Write program code that picks each of the following random numbers.

   (i)  A whole number between 0 and 4 inclusive.

   (ii) A whole number between 0 and 100 inclusive.

(iii) A whole number between 1 and 12 inclusive.

(iv) A whole number between 20 and 30 inclusive.

(v) A whole number which is 5, 10 or 15.

**Marks 2, 5**

## QUESTION 4

A programmer is writing part of a program which enters the number of living grandparents a child has. The number is validated to be in the range 0 to 4.

The programmer tests the code by entering '3', which is accepted by the program. The programmer then concludes that the programming is correct.

**(a)** Explain why the programmer cannot be sure that the program is correct without further testing.

**(b)** Supply two other sets of test data that would test the program more fully, and give a reason why you chose each set of data.

**Marks 2, 2**

---

## ANSWER TO QUESTION 1

**(a)** Concatenation is joining string variables together to make longer strings.

**(b)** STRING data type.

**(c)** The ampersand symbol (&) is typically used to concatenate strings.

**(d)** (i)  Molly Miller

    (ii) Mrs Miller B.Sc.

## ANSWER TO QUESTION 2

**(a)** The LEN function returns the number of characters in a STRING.

The ROUND function rounds a number to a specified number of decimal places.

**(b)** (i)  LEN("Hello")

        Returns 5

    (ii)  LEN("Mr President")

        Returns 12

   (iii) LEN("Good" & " " & "boy.")

        Returns 9

   (iv) ROUND(34·619, 1)

        Returns 34·6

   (v)  ROUND(0·087803, 2)

        Returns 0·09

   (vi) ROUND(50·3175, 3)

        Returns 50·318

**(c)** SQR, SIN, COS, TAN, LEFT, RIGHT, MID, etc.

---

## ANSWER TO QUESTION 3

**(a)** (i)  This instruction picks a random integer number between 0 and 51 inclusive.

    (ii)  This could be used in a computer card game to pick a card from a deck of 52 playing cards.

**(b)** (i)  X = Int(Rnd * 5)

    (ii)  X = Int(Rnd * 101)

   (iii) X = Int(Rnd * 12) + 1

   (iv) X = Int(Rnd * 11) + 20

   (v)  X = (Int(Rnd * 3) + 1) * 5

## ANSWER TO QUESTION 4

**(a)** Just because the program works for 3 grandparents does not mean that it will work for all possible cases. The program should be tested with extreme numbers which lie on the boundaries, or with exceptional data.

**(b)** Test data 1

    Grandparents = 4

    This is to test whether the program works on the extremities of valid data.

    (Grandparents = 0 could be chosen for the same reason.)

    Test data 2

    Grandparents = 7

    This is to test whether the program works with exceptional data that is outwith the possible values. (Other examples of exceptional data could be Grandparents = –3, Grandparents = Ted etc.)

# QUESTIONS AND ANSWERS 4

## QUESTION 1

Programs are tested to locate and remove any errors.

**(a)** Errors can be classified as syntax, execution or logic errors.

Describe each of these three types of error.

**(b)** Which type of error is present in each of the following pieces of programming code?

A    Let Area = Length + Breadth

B    Let MyShare = PrizeMoney / 0

C    Let NetSalary = Tax – GrossSalary

D    Let Average = Score1 + Score2 / 2

E    Ify Age > 21 Then Suitable = False

**Marks 3, 5**

## QUESTION 2

A program enters the age of a man and the age of his dog.

The program then calculates and displays the age of the dog in human years and also displays the age of the man.

The program then displays a message saying whether the man is older, the dog is older or they are both the same age in human years. (1 dog year equals 7 human years.)

**(a)** Write down three sets of test data that could be used to thoroughly test the program, and give a reason why you chose each set of test data.

**(b)** What output should each set of test data display?

**Marks 6, 3**

## QUESTION 3

Most computer software requires modification at some point in the future.

A program that is readable is easier to modify in the future than one which is not.

**(a)** Explain the term 'readable' as applied to a computer program.

**(b)** Explain the term 'white space' as applied to a program listing.

**(c)** Some programs need modification because they crash easily when given invalid input.

What word is used to describe a program that does not crash easily when unexpected input is entered?

**Marks 1,1,1**

# QUESTION 4

A program enters the name of an animal and its life expectancy in years.

The life expectancy is validated to be in the range 1 to 150.

The program then displays a message stating whether the animal has a short, medium or long life expectancy. (Short = under 20 years, Medium = 20 to 60 years, Long = over 60 years.)

Pseudocode illustrating the design of the program logic is shown below.

Suggest how meaningful identifiers and indentation can be used to make the program design more readable.

```
RECEIVE a FROM KEYBOARD
REPEAT
RECEIVE b FROM KEYBOARD
IF b < 1 OR b > 150 THEN
SEND ["That can't be the right life expectancy!"] TO DISPLAY
END IF
UNTIL b > 0 AND b < 151
IF b < 20 THEN
SEND [a, " has a short life expectancy."] TO DISPLAY
END IF
IF b >= 20 AND b <= 60 Then
SEND [a, " has a medium life expectancy."] TO DISPLAY
END IF
IF b > 60 THEN
SEND [a, " has a long life expectancy."] TO DISPLAY
END IF
```

**Marks 2**

## ANSWER TO QUESTION 1

**(a)** Syntax errors are errors which break the rules of the language, such as misspelling a command word.

Execution errors are errors detected during the running of the program, such as dividing by zero, which is not possible mathematically.

Logic errors are errors in the logic of the code itself, such as subtracting two numbers the wrong way round.

**(b)** A  Logic error, since Area should be Length times Breadth.

B  Execution error, since you can't divide by zero.

C  Logic error, since NetSalary should be GrossSalary – Tax.

D  Logic error, since Average should be (Score1 – Score2) / 2.

E  Syntax error, since If has been misspelt as Ify.

## ANSWER TO QUESTION 2

**(a)** Test data 1
Dog age = 3, Human age = 15
This data is chosen to test the situation where the dog is older than the man in human years.

Test data 2
Dog age = 7, Human age = 60
This data is chosen to test the situation where the man is older than the dog in human years.

Test data 3
Dog age = 5, Human age = 35
This data is chosen to test the situation where the dog and the man are the same age in human years.

## ANSWER TO QUESTION 3

**(a)** Readability means that the program code is easy to follow and understand.

**(b)** White space is blank lines and indentations in the code to make procedures and program constructs easier to take in visually.

**(c)** Robust.

## ANSWER TO QUESTION 4

The variable names can be changed into meaningful identifiers such as Animal_Name and Life_Expectancy instead of a and b.

The IFs and the REPEAT ... UNTIL ... loop can be indented to make the instructions stand out more.

**(b)** Test 1 output
Dog's human age 21, Man's age 15. The dog is older.

Test 2 output
Dog's human age 49, Man's age 60. The man is older.

Test 3 output
Dog's human age 35, Man's age 35. They are the same age.

# DATA REPRESENTATION 1

ON    OFF

## BINARY NUMBERS

A computer is a **two-state** device in that it uses electric charges set to two different values (ON or OFF) to store data and program instructions. Just like an electric light bulb, the charge can be represented by a 1 for ON and a 0 for OFF.

The data stored on a computer can be represented by **binary numbers**, which are made up of the two digits 1 and 0. Human beings find it harder to work with binary numbers than with the decimal number system that we are used to for representing numbers and performing calculations.

## UNITS

The following units of storage are used to represent the sizes of files and the capacity of storage devices on computer systems:

| | |
|---|---|
| A **bit** is a binary digit. | (1 or 0) |
| A **byte** is a group of 8 bits. | (for example 10111011) |
| A **kilobyte** (Kb) is 1,024 bytes. | ($2^{10}$ bytes) |
| A **megabyte** (Mb) is 1,024 kilobytes = 1,048,576 bytes. | ($2^{20}$ bytes) |
| A **gigabyte** (GB) is 1,024 megabytes = 1,073,741,824 bytes. | ($2^{30}$ bytes) |
| A **terabyte** (Tb) is 1,024 gigabytes = 1,099,511,627,776 bytes. | ($2^{40}$ bytes) |
| A **petabyte** (Pb) is 1,024 terabytes = 1,125,899,906,842,624 bytes. | ($2^{50}$ bytes) |

There are units of storage larger than a petabyte. Use a search engine to find the names and the capacities of the next three units.

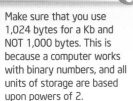

**DON'T FORGET**

Make sure that you use 1,024 bytes for a Kb and NOT 1,000 bytes. This is because a computer works with binary numbers, and all units of storage are based upon powers of 2.

## POSITIVE NUMBERS

Positive whole numbers are represented in a computer system in the binary number system. The binary number system uses units of twos, fours, eights, sixteens etc. to represent a number instead of the units of tens, hundreds, thousands etc. used in the decimal system.

**EXAMPLE 1:**

The number 76 is represented by 01001100:

```
128  64  32  16  8  4  2  1
 0   1   0   0  1  1  0  0   = 64 + 8 + 4 = 76.
```

**EXAMPLE 2:**

The number 155 is represented by 10011011:

```
128  64  32  16  8  4  2  1
 1   0   0   1  1  0  1  1   = 128 + 16 + 8 + 2 + 1 = 155.
```

**VIDEO**

Head online and watch the clip for a further explanation of how to convert a binary number to a decimal: www.brightredbooks.net/ N5Computing

contd

## Changing decimal numbers to binary

The method shown here is used to convert a decimal number into binary. The example converts the number 213 into binary.

The number 213 is repeatedly divided by 2 until it is reduced to 0.

Write down the remainders for each division. The remainders (read from bottom to top) give the binary number.
Answer = 11010101.

| 2 | 213 | |
|---|-----|-----|
| 2 | 106 | R 1 |
| 2 | 53  | R 0 |
| 2 | 26  | R 1 |
| 2 | 13  | R 0 |
| 2 | 6   | R 1 |
| 2 | 3   | R 0 |
| 2 | 1   | R 1 |
|   | 0   | R 1 |

**ONLINE TEST**

Test yourself on numbers in data representation online at www.brightredbooks.net/N5Computing

# REAL NUMBERS

Real numbers include positive and negative whole numbers and numbers which have a decimal fraction part. Numbers such as 6·7, –0·0035, 7·0, 89 and 562·37 are all examples of real numbers.

Computers use a system called **floating-point notation** to represent these numbers. A floating-point number is made up of a decimal fraction part called the **mantissa** and a power part called the **exponent**.

**EXAMPLE:**

$$\underset{\downarrow}{\text{Mantissa}} \qquad \underset{\downarrow}{\text{Exponent}}$$

$$10110110101110101 = 0{\cdot}1011011 \times 2^{10001}$$

For example, a floating-point number which uses 16 bits for the mantissa and 8 bits for the exponent is less accurate and stores a smaller range of numbers than a floating-point number that uses 24 bits for the mantissa and 16 bits for the exponent.

Advantage = extremely large and small numbers can be represented in a relatively small number of bits.

Disadvantage = the number is less accurate because the mantissa is rounded off to a set number of significant figures.

**DON'T FORGET**

The accuracy of a floating-point number is increased by allocating more bits to the mantissa. The range of numbers that can be stored is increased by allocating more bits to the exponent.

## THINGS TO DO AND THINK ABOUT

The hexadecimal number system is used in computing as well as the binary number system. Go to the internet site www.techterms.com and find out why the hexadecimal number system is important in computing.

**DON'T FORGET**

Computers use different systems to store different types of numbers. Positive numbers, integers and real numbers are stored as binary numbers, two's complement numbers and floating-point numbers respectively.

# DATA REPRESENTATION 2

## CHARACTERS

Text data is stored in many types of program on a computer. For example, word-processing, databases and websites all require to store textual information. Text is stored on a computer by representing each individual character as a unique binary code. The characters include letters (upper and lower case), numeric digits (0 to 9), punctuation marks (?, &, !, £ etc.) and mathematical operations (+, −, *, / etc.).

### ASCII (American Standard Code for Information Interchange)

Standards for text representation have been developed so that different programs using the same codes can interpret data as the same characters.

**ASCII** is a common standard for representing text that uses an 8-bit (1-byte) code for each character. For example, the letter E is stored as 01000101 (or 69 in decimal), and the character £ is stored as 00100011 (or 35 in decimal).

There are 32 special character codes known as control characters. **Control characters** are special non-printing characters in a character set, used for special purposes. Examples of control characters are Return, Tab and End of file.

### Extended ASCII code

The standard ASCII code system can represent 128 different characters because it uses 7 bits for the character code while the 8th bit is used for error detection.

Extended ASCII code uses all 8 bits for the character code and can represent 256 characters that include symbols such as € (Euro), ½ (half), © (copyright), μ (micro unit) and so on.

### Character set

A character set is the complete list of characters that a computer system can represent.

This includes uppercase letters, lowercase letters, punctuation symbols, numeric symbols and control characters.

## BIT-MAPPED GRAPHICS

The tiny dots that make up a bit-mapped graphic image are called **pixels**. The word 'pixel' comes from the term 'picture element', since the pixels are the elementary parts of a picture.

### Bit depth

A **bit-mapped** graphics program stores the data in a two-dimensional grid of pixels. A binary code is used to represent the colour of each pixel. In a black-and-white image where each pixel can be only two states, black can be represented by a 1 and white by a 0. In an image with lots of colours, several bits are required for the colour code to represent all the different colours. The **bit depth** is the number of bits used for the colour code. Using 24 bits for the colour code of each pixel is quite common, as over 16 million different colours can be represented, which is at the limit of the number of colours that the human eye can distinguish.

Black and white

Colour

**DON'T FORGET**

The number of bits used to represent the colour of each pixel is called the bit depth. The higher the bit depth, the more colours that can be represented.

contd

### Resolution

This is the number of pixels in a fixed area of a bit-mapped graphic.

High-**resolution** images have a large number of small pixels, and low-resolution images have a small number of large pixels.

High-resolution graphics have a better quality than low-resolution graphics but require more storage since there are more pixels in the image.

The resolution of graphics is normally measured in d.p.i. (dots per inch).

## VECTOR GRAPHICS

**Vector graphics** is a type of graphics that stores the image as a collection of objects such as rectangles, circles, lines, triangles and so on. The attributes of each object are stored, such as coordinates, length, breadth, fill colour and so on.

**EXAMPLE:**

| Object | Attributes |
|---|---|
| Rectangle | start x, start y, length, breadth, fill red, line green, and so on. |
| Ellipse | centre x, centre y, radius x, radius y, fill red, line black, and so on. |
| Line | start x, start y, end x, end y, line blue, and so on. |
| Polygon | point1 x, point1 y, point2 x, point2 y, point3 x, point3 y, fill green, line blue, and so on. |

## COMPARISON OF BIT-MAPPED GRAPHICS AND VECTOR GRAPHICS

There are advantages and disadvantages that each type of graphics program has over others.

| | Bit-Mapped Graphics | Vector Graphics |
|---|---|---|
| File size | The file size of bit-mapped graphics is large, since the colour code of thousands or even millions of pixels must be stored. | The file size of vector graphics is generally small, since only the objects and their attributes are stored, not pixels. |
| Editing | A bit-mapped image is edited at the pixel level. | Vector graphics are edited at an attribute level, for example changing the length of a rectangle or the line colour of a circle. Also, overlapping objects can be separated again, which cannot be done with bit-mapped graphics since the image is not stored as objects. |
| Fine detail | Bit-mapped graphics allow the editing of fine detail in photos taken by digital cameras. For example, the program Photoshop uses techniques such as airbrushing to produce the finished photographs shown in magazines, brochures and leaflets. | This kind of fine detail is not possible in vector graphics because the image is made up of shapes such as rectangles and lines. |
| Enlarging | If a bit-mapped image is enlarged, then it becomes jagged. | The resolution of a vector graphic image is NOT fixed by the resolution of the pixels, so that an enlarged image does NOT become jagged. |

 **ONLINE**

Use a search engine to look up the features of the program Photoshop, using keywords such as 'Photoshop', 'editing', 'basics', 'tutorial' and so on.

 **DON'T FORGET**

You probably have both types of graphics program on your computer. The graphics program Paint is an example of bit-mapped graphics, whereas the drawing toolbar in Microsoft Word is an example of vector graphics.

 **ONLINE TEST**

Test yourself on graphics online at www.brightredbooks.net/N5Computing

 ## THINGS TO DO AND THINK ABOUT

Bit-mapped graphics and vector graphics are two types of graphics software. Each stores and edits the image in different ways. Make sure that you learn the differences and the advantages and disadvantages of each type of software.

# COMPUTER STRUCTURE

## COMPUTER SYSTEM

The diagram alongside shows the components of a computer system. All computers work in essentially the same way. Input devices are used to enter data, which is processed by a central processing unit, and then the results are displayed by output devices.

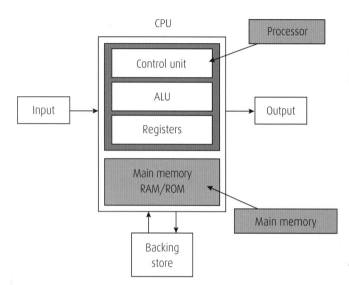

Input is performed by devices such as keyboards, scanners and digital cameras. Output is performed by devices such as flat screens and printers.

The **CPU** (central processing unit) consists of a processor chip and main memory which is made up of RAM and ROM chips.

Backing store devices are used to permanently store programs and data.

**Peripheral** is a term that is used to describe **input**, **output** and **backing store** devices that are connected to the CPU. Keyboards, USB flash memory and printers are examples of peripheral devices.

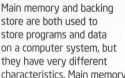

**DON'T FORGET**

Make sure that you know the basic diagram of a computer system and understand the function of the labelled parts.

**DON'T FORGET**

Main memory and backing store are both used to store programs and data on a computer system, but they have very different characteristics. Main memory has much less capacity than backing store and does not store data permanently.

## PROCESSOR

The processor chip has three basic components. These are the control unit, arithmetic logic unit and registers.

### Control unit

The **control unit** manages the execution of program instructions by fetching them one at a time from main memory. The control unit has complex electronic circuits that allow instructions to be decoded and executed. Signals are sent out by the processor to initiate events within the CPU.

### Arithmetic logic unit

The **ALU** performs arithmetic operations such as addition, subtraction, multiplication and division, and logical decisions such as AND, OR and NOT.

### Registers

The processor has individual storage locations called **registers** that temporarily store items of data. For example, the accumulator is a register that stores the results of calculations performed in the ALU. Another processor register is the instruction register, which holds the program instruction that is currently being decoded and executed.

# MEMORY

**Main memory** is used to temporarily store programs while they are being run. It is part of the central processing unit and consists of **RAM** and **ROM** chips.

RAM (Random-Access Memory) can be written to and read from. It loses its contents when power is switched off.

ROM (Read-Only Memory) can be read from but not written to. It does not lose its contents when power is switched off. ROM is used to permanently store programs that are important to the system, such as the BIOS, which loads the operating system from disc when the computer is started up.

When the power is switched off, the data that has been entered into RAM will be lost. Backing store is used to permanently store data that otherwise would be lost.

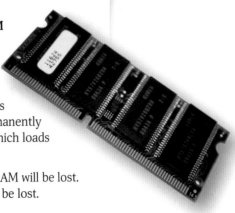

# ADDRESSABILITY OF MAIN MEMORY

Main memory is made up of thousands of millions of storage locations, each of which is used to hold program instructions and data.

Each memory location is given a unique address so that the processor can identify it.

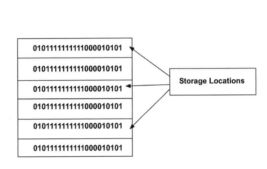

# BUSES

A bus is a set of parallel wires which connect the processor with main memory. The buses are used to move data between the processor and main memory locations and to specify the address of memory locations to be used.

## Address bus

The **address bus** is used to specify which memory location is to be used to read data from or to write data to.

## Data bus

The **data bus** is used to carry data from a memory location to the processor and vice versa. It is a two-way bus.

## Control bus

The **control bus** is used to send out signals to initiate events such as reading an item of data from a memory location into the processor or writing an item of data from the processor to a memory location.

**ONLINE**

Use a search engine to find out other control-bus functions apart from Read and Write.

**ONLINE TEST**

Visit www.brightredbooks.net/N5Computing for a test on computer stucture.

## THINGS TO DO AND THINK ABOUT

All computer systems have the same basic structure. They have a processor, memory and buses which work together to execute programs. They also have input, output and storage devices to enter, display and permanently store data. The next time you are sitting at a computer, try to list the input, output and storage devices being used.

# TRANSLATION OF HIGH-LEVEL LANGUAGES

## MACHINE CODE

**Machine code** is the computer's own programming language, which uses binary codes to represent the program instructions and data.

Machine-code programs are very difficult for humans to write, and it is easy to make mistakes, since all instructions are made up of patterns of 1s and 0s. Writing machine-code programs is very time-consuming, since the instructions are very simple and it requires many of these instructions to do even simple tasks such as working out the average of a small list of numbers. It is also very hard to find and correct errors in machine-code programs.

Shown below is part of a machine-code program.

```
10111001        00110010 0101001
01000010        101110 101010110
11001110        0100110011110011
01010111        1100010110110101
```

## HIGH-LEVEL LANGUAGES

In the early days of computing, all programs were written in machine code. **High-level languages** were developed to make the process of software development easier and quicker. Today, almost all software is written in a high-level language.

Shown below is an example of a program written in a high-level language.

The program asks for the name and age of a dog and then displays the equivalent human age.

```
'Declare variables
Dim DogName As String
Dim DogAge As Integer
Dim HumanAge As Integer
'Get the dog data from TextBoxes
Let DogName = Text1.Text
Let DogAge = Val(Text2.Text)
'Calculate the equivalent human age of the dog
If DogAge < 4 Then
    Let HumanAge = DogAge * 7
Else
    Let HumanAge = 21 + 4 * (DogAge - 3)
End If
'Display a suitable message
Picture1.Print "Dog's age: "; DogAge
Picture1.Print "If "; DogName; " was a human he/she
would be "; HumanAge; " years old."
End Sub

Private Sub Command2_Click()
'Clear the display
Picture1.Cls
End Sub

Private Sub Command3_Click()
'End the program
End
```

**ONLINE**

Use a search engine to investigate different high-level languages and the purposes for which they were created. Use keywords such as 'High-level language', 'Java', 'Visual Basic', 'HTML' and so on.

contd

## Advantages of high-level languages

1   The commands use English keywords such as PRINT, INPUT, REPEAT etc. which are easy to understand and remember.

2   Complex arithmetic can be performed in one instruction that would take many machine-code instructions.
For example: Let Volume = 3·14 * Radius ^ 2 * Height
For example: Let Hypotenuse = SQR(Side1 ^ 2 + Side2 ^ 2)

3   They have inbuilt mathematical and logical functions to process the data.
For example: Let Length = Cos(Angle) * 4
For example: Let Initial = Left(Name, 1)

4   One high-level instruction can perform the same processing as lots of machine-code instructions.

5   The program can be broken down into subprograms (functions and procedures) to produce modular code.

# TRANSLATORS

All high-level-language programs must be translated into machine code before they can be run. One high-level-language instruction generally translates into several machine-code instructions.

## Compilers

A **compiler** translates the complete program in one go before the program is run.

1   The compiled program runs fast, since there is no translation at run time.
(It has been translated before it is run.)

2   It produces a stand-alone machine-code program which runs by itself without the need for the source code and the compiler.

3   The source program will only be used again if the program needs to be changed.

4   Errors in the source code are only identified when the program is compiled.
Once the errors have been corrected, the complete program has to be compiled again before it can be run and tested.

## Interpreters

An **interpreter** translates and executes a program one statement at a time while the program is run.

1   Because the interpreter translates statements as it executes the program (this takes time), it will run more slowly than a compiled program which has been compiled into machine code before it is run.

2   The interpreter must also be in memory as the program is executed, whereas a compiler is not needed once the program has been compiled. Thus an interpreted program requires more memory than the compiled version of the same program.

3   The interpreter is a simpler (and hence less expensive) program.

4   Interpreted programs are easier to edit than compiled programs, since the program will run up to the point of error and can then be corrected and run again immediately, whereas a compiled program requires the complete program to be compiled again before it can be run.

**DON'T FORGET**

A compiler and an interpreter are two types of programs used to translate high-level languages into machine code. You should know the difference in how each translator operates and the advantages and disadvantages of each.

**ONLINE TEST**

How well have you learned about the translation of high-level languages? Check online at www.brightredbooks.net/ N5Computing

## THINGS TO DO AND THINK ABOUT

All computers execute machine code, which is binary patterns that can be executed by a processor chip. High-level languages exist to make it easier for a human to write programs, but a compiler or an interpreter must be used to translate the code into machine code before it can be run.

# ENVIRONMENTAL IMPACT

## ENERGY USE

How much electricity do computers use?

A typical **desktop computer** uses about 100 to 250 watts, which is considerably more than a laptop computer, which uses around 20 to 60 watts. If a computer is on the internet and making intensive use of its processor and disc drives, then it will consume much more energy than a computer that is offline and performing tasks that are less demanding of the system. It can be calculated that a typical desktop computer being used for 8 hours a day would use about 500 kilowatt hours in one year. At a current cost of around 10p per kilowatt hour, this would amount to a cost of £50 a year.

### ONLINE

Go to the website www. electricity-usage.com and use the calculator to explore how much energy your computer and peripheral devices use.

## CARBON FOOTPRINT

There is some debate about how much greenhouse gases are contributing to global warming. However, it is generally accepted that emissions of **greenhouse gases**, in particular carbon dioxide, make a serious contribution to climate change.

**Carbon footprint** is a measure of how much carbon dioxide is produced in the making or use of devices such as televisions, cars, aircraft and computing equipment.

The manufacture of IT equipment contributes to the carbon footprint. The making of a single desktop computer requires the burning of 10 times its own weight in fossil fuel.

Using computing equipment uses electricity, which is largely produced in power stations by burning fossil fuels such as coal and oil. The waste product of this process is the creation of large amounts of carbon dioxide.

On the other hand, in some respects the use of IT can help to reduce the carbon footprint. For example, the increasing number of people working from home decreases the need for travel. Cars, buses and trains all burn a large amount of fossil fuels.

Another example is that of **video conferencing**, where meetings take place in a virtual conference using online computers and multimedia hardware devices. Traditional meetings in hotels and conference centres can require air travel, which has a large carbon footprint.

## REDUCING POWER CONSUMPTION

In the past, computers were left on full power, sometimes overnight, when not being used, which was a complete waste of enormous amounts of electricity.

If a computer was not used for a period of time, it was often set to start a screensaver, which also used up power to run the screensaver program.

Modern computers have settings to give control over their power usage and have consequently considerably reduced their power consumption.

contd

## Settings on monitors

Monitors use up a great deal of power, especially large ones with the brightness turned up high.

Settings can be used to reduce the amount of power being used.

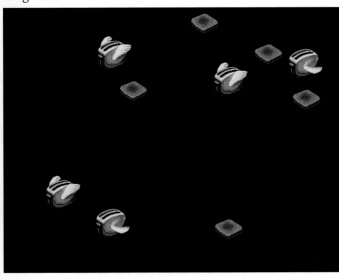

- The brightness level can be set that is appropriate to the brightness level of the environment. If it's brighter than it needs to be, then it is using up more power than is necessary.

- Monitors can be set to automatically go into sleep mode when not being used for a set period of time, typically 15 minutes or so.

## Shutdown settings

When a computer is shut down, all of the programs and data are closed and the computer shuts down the operating system. A computer that's shut down uses almost no power. Some components such as an internal clock may retain a small amount of power.

Settings can be used to specify the amount of time after which the computer will shut down when not being used.

However, when the computer is to be used again, it needs to be restarted to reboot the operating system and initialise hardware, which can take a few minutes.

## Standby/sleep mode

In standby or sleep mode, the computer enters a low-power state which keeps the computer's data in memory but other parts of the computer are switched off and won't use any power. When the computer is turned back on, it is it ready to use in a few seconds since it does not have to boot up, and the user can start from where they left off.

Settings can be used to specify the period of inactivity after which the computer will go into standby mode.

Standby is useful when the computer is not being used for a small amount of time. However, it uses more power than shutting down the computer completely.

## THINGS TO DO AND THINK ABOUT

The manufacture, use and disposal of IT hardware have consequences for the environment. They use up the world's resources, cause pollution and leave a carbon footprint which is contributing towards global warming. Steps to reduce these effects include developing computers that consume less energy and the recycling of hardware components. Look around your house or classroom and identify things that you already do or could improve on to reduce your energy use.

### DON'T FORGET

Apart from carbon dioxide, there are other gases that contribute towards climate change. Nitrogen trifluoride ($NF_3$) is a waste product from factories that make flat-screen displays. This gas is more harmful in warming the atmosphere than carbon dioxide but is produced in much smaller amounts.

### ONLINE TEST

Test yourself on the environmental impact of computing online at www.brightredbooks.net/N5Computing

# SECURITY PRECAUTIONS

## SECURITY RISKS

There are many risks to computer systems such as virus attacks, hacking, identity theft, online fraud, keylogging, phishing and so on.

To protect against these threats, there are a range of products such as anti-virus software, firewalls, passwords, biometrics and so on that help to keep computer systems, and their users, safe.

## ANTI-VIRUS SOFTWARE

**Anti-virus software** scans a computer system to detect and remove viruses. Viruses can be identified if they have a known pattern of instructions or if the virus program is performing some suspicious activity such as copying the contents of an e-mail address book in order to spread to other computers. Since new viruses are constantly being created, it is important to regularly update the anti-virus software so that it will recognise these new viruses. Many anti-virus software programs also protect against other types of harmful software such as **spyware** and **adware** which can irritatingly display advertisements on your computer.

## FIREWALLS

A **firewall** protects a computer system from damage from unauthorised users by filtering all incoming and outgoing internet traffic through a firewall computer. It does this by analysing the packets of data being transmitted and determining whether they should be allowed through or not. Thus only known and trusted users are permitted to access the data on the computer system. Firewalls can also control which websites a computer can access on the internet.

Individual home computers can be protected with a firewall to improve security on the internet. Companies will protect their networks using a network firewall.

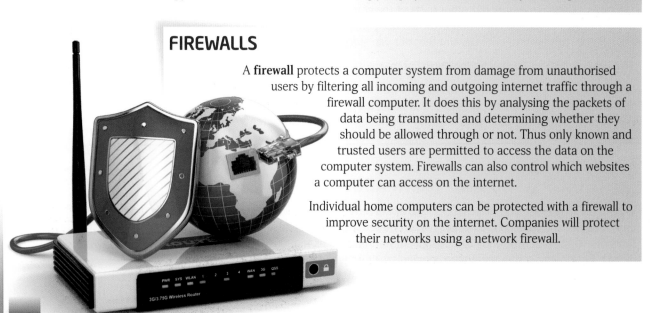

# ENCRYPTION

The word 'encryption' comes from the Greek word 'kryptos', meaning hidden or secret.

Encryption is the process of protecting data by using an encryption key to put it into code so that if it can't be understood if it is accessed by someone who should not be viewing it.

In electronic communication, data is often encrypted so that if it is intercepted then it can't be viewed unless it is decrypted by the correct key.

Secure websites and sensitive data such as passwords and credit-card details are encrypted so that they can't be read without the correct decoding key.

# PASSWORDS AND BIOMETRICS

## Passwords

User accounts on networks and stand-alone computers can be protected with **passwords**. Usually, a username is required to log on, as well as a password to provide extra security. Individual files such as word-processing and spreadsheet documents can also be given a password which is needed to open the file.

Some passwords are case-sensitive, which means that the password distinguishes between uppercase and lowercase letters.

Passwords should be chosen wisely so that it is hard for other people to discover or guess your password. Using a mixture of random uppercase letters, lowercase letters, digits and punctuation characters makes for a strong password. Some people pick weak passwords such as the name of their pet, friend, football team and so on, or a password that is too short and is easily discovered by other people who can then hack into their account. For example, the password R3jK942f is much stronger than the password Vegas.

## Biometrics

This is a form of security system based on the detection and recognition of human physical characteristics. Common examples are retinal scans, fingerprints and voice and face recognition. These characteristics are unique to a human being and so are very difficult to forge. Some systems require the input of a username and password as well as some form of **biometric** scan to provide extra security.

# SECURITY SUITES

A **security suite** is a group of utility programs that protect a computer from viruses and other malware. Anti-virus software and firewalls are the main functions of most security suites. However, other functions are usually provided such as parental controls, protection against identity theft, and password protection of data storage.

Some security suites offer more types of protection than others which are limited in their protection. It is also important that the security suite is updated regularly to guard against the latest malware threats.

 ## THINGS TO DO AND THINK ABOUT

There are many threats to the security of a computer system from which the users need to be protected. These include threats from viruses or hackers, and protecting children from access to unwanted material on the internet. Passwords, encryption, biometrics, firewalls and so on are all means of protecting a computer system and keeping the data being held secure.

 **DON'T FORGET**

It is important to change your password regularly. If it is stolen, there will then be less time in which it can be used to access your private information or to do damage.

 **ONLINE**

Research the functions provided by different types of security suites on the internet. Norton and McAfee are two companies that make security suites.

 **ONLINE TEST**

Test yourself on security precautions at www.brightredbooks.net/N5Computing

# QUESTIONS AND ANSWERS 1

## INTRODUCTION

The following questions are based on the work of the Computer Systems area of study.

They are intended to be similar to the level and style of questions that you can expect in the exam.

## QUESTION 1

**(a)** Wendy is a student in an architecture college. She uses a CD with a storage capacity of 780 Mb to back up her data. How many CDs would be needed to store the same amount of data as a 16 GB USB memory stick?

**(b)** Wendy is filling in a form for a job application on a computer and enters her street address as 1 Beachfront Avenue.

Explain how the computer stores the text for the address.

**(c)** A logo for a clothes shop was created using a graphics software package.

The blue rectangle is to be made larger. Explain why it is easier to do the editing in a vector graphics package than in a bit-mapped graphics package.

**Marks 2, 2, 2**

## QUESTION 2

Gregg is using a programming language which uses two representations to store floating-point numbers.

Notation A    16-bit exponent    16-bit mantissa
Notation B    8-bit exponent     24-bit mantissa

**(a)** Describe the terms 'mantissa' and 'exponent'.

**(b)** Gregg needs to store the floating-point numbers accurately in his program.

State which notation he should choose, and justify your answer.

**(c)** What would be the effect on the floating-point numbers that are stored in Notation A if the exponent was stored in 24 bits?

**Marks 2, 2, 1**

## QUESTION 3

Sam is writing a book of fairy stories for an e-book which can display the text in seven different languages.

**(a)** Explain how ASCII code is used to store the following piece of text in binary.

Once upon a time ...

**(b)** Explain the difference between extended ASCII and standard ASCII code.

**(c)** What name is given to non-printing characters such as RETURN and TAB?

**(d)** How many bytes of storage would be required to store the following sentence in ASCII code?

After all, tomorrow is another day.

**Marks 1, 1, 1, 2**

# QUESTION 4

Rosie uses a computer to design posters for a marketing company.

**(a)** Rosie has just produced a poster but is concerned that the file has a very high capacity.

Describe **two** ways in which Rosie can reduce the file size.

**(b)** Why do bit-mapped graphics files usually have a higher capacity than vector graphics files?

**(c)** The image shown alongside was enlarged in a graphics package. State whether bit-mapped or vector graphics were used to create the image, and justify your answer.

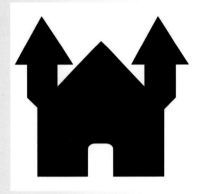 

**Marks 2, 2, 2**

## ANSWER TO QUESTION 1

**(a)** 16 gigabytes = 16 × 1,024 megabytes = 16,384 megabytes.

The number of CDs = 16,384 / 780 = 21.

**(b)** The computer stores each character in a unique binary code. A standard is ASCII, which represents each character in an 8-bit code.

**(c)** A vector graphics package stores the rectangle as an object which can be easily selected and resized. If it was a bit-mapped package, then the rectangle would have to be erased and then redrawn.

## ANSWER TO QUESTION 2

**(a)** The mantissa is the fractional part of a floating-point number that stores the significant figures of the number.

The exponent is the power part of the number.

For example, 1011010101110101 = 0·101011 × 2^17

$$\underset{\text{Mantissa}}{\uparrow} \qquad \underset{\text{Exponent}}{\uparrow}$$

**(b)** Gregg should choose Notation B, since it is more accurate because it uses more bits to store the mantissa, which gives more significant figures and hence more accuracy.

**(c)** Notation A would be able to store a larger range of numbers, since the power can be made higher.

## ANSWER TO QUESTION 3

**(a)** Each character is stored in an 8-bit binary code (including the spaces).

**(b)** Standard ASCII is essentially a 7-bit code and can represent 128 characters, whereas extended ASCII is an 8-bit code and can represent 256 different characters.

**(c)** These are examples of control characters.

**(d)** Each character requires 2 bytes of storage.

The sentence requires 70 bytes (28 letters, 5 spaces, a comma and a full stop) of storage.

## ANSWER TO QUESTION 4

**(a)** Reduce the resolution of the image.

Reduce the bit depth of the image.

Use file compression to reduce the file size.

**(b)** Bit-mapped graphics files are high-capacity because they need to store the colour code of thousands if not millions of pixels.

Vector graphics do not store pixels but just a list of objects with their attributes.

**(c)** It was created with a bit-mapped graphics package.

The colour codes for the pixels are stored, and so the pixels become jagged and chunky when enlarged.

This would not happen in a vector graphics package because only the attributes of the objects would change, and the size of the pixels is not a factor.

# QUESTIONS AND ANSWERS 2

## QUESTION 1

Shown below are sections of code from two computer programs.

State which type of language has been used to write each section of code.

**(a)**

**Program 1**
```
Student = Text1.Text
Score = Text2.Text
If Score < 50 Then Label1.Text = "Fail."
If Score > 49 And Score < 60 Then Label1.Text = "C Pass."
If Score > 59 And Score < 70 Then Label1.Text = "B Pass."
If Score > 69 And Score < 100 Then Label1.Text = "A Pass."
```

**(b)**

**Program 2**
```
0011001011011111    1101101100110010
0011011100000110    1011100011010101
0000011111001111    0111110100001101
1110001010101101    1000111100001111
```

Marks 1, 1

## QUESTION 2

High-level languages require a compiler or an interpreter to translate the program.

**(a)** Which of the following statements are true about interpreters and compilers?

A  Interpreted programs run faster than compiled programs.

B  A compiled program uses up less memory than an interpreted program.

C  They both produce object code.

D  It is easier to correct errors in an interpreted program than in a compiled program.

E  They both translate high-level languages into machine code.

F  Both an interpreted and a compiled program are translated before they are executed.

**(b)** The computer programmer in an astrology department in a university has written software to process data collected from their telescopes. After 6 months, the astronomers realise that there are errors in the program. The programmer has a copy of the program's object code but not the source code.

(i) Which type of translator was used to produce this program?

(ii) Can the program be changed to correct the errors? Explain your answer.

Marks 6, 2

**DON'T FORGET**

It is a common fault to answer your own question instead of the exam question. Read the preamble for the question carefully and be sure that you are answering the requirements of the questions. For example, if asked to compare two processes, don't just give a description of each process.

## QUESTION 3

At one time, all computer programs were written in machine code. Nowadays, almost all software is written in a high-level language.

**(a)** Why is it difficult and time-consuming to write programs in machine code?

**(b)** Give two features of high-level languages.

**(c)** At one time, documents were produced in offices by secretaries using typewriters.

Computer programs such as word-processors and databases are now used in offices to create and organise data.

Give one environmental impact resulting from the introduction of computer programs in offices.

Marks 2, 2, 1

# QUESTION 4

Shown below is a diagram of a computer system.

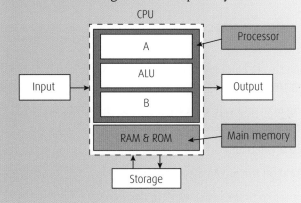

(a) What function does the ALU perform apart from arithmetic calculations?

(b) Name the two other components of the processor, A and B.

(c) Main memory is made up of two types, RAM and ROM. A data file is loaded into main memory to be edited.

State whether the data file is stored in RAM or ROM, and explain your answer.

(d) The processor has three buses to connect it with main memory.

Describe the functions of the three buses.

**Marks 1, 2, 2, 3**

## ANSWER TO QUESTION 4

(a) The ALU performs logical decisions (AND, OR, NOT) as well as calculations.

(b) The other two components are the control unit and registers.

(c) The data file is loaded into RAM (Random-Access Memory)
RAM can be written to, but ROM can only be read from and not written to.

(d) The address bus specifies which memory location to read data from or write data to.
The control bus sends out signals to initiate events such as reading or writing data.
The data bus is used to carry data from a memory location to the processor and vice versa.

## ANSWER TO QUESTION 3

(a) Machine-code instructions are in binary code, so it is very easy to make mistakes with the codes; and reading code to make changes and locate errors is fraught with difficulty. Also, a single machine-code instruction does very little processing, and it takes many instructions to perform the same amount of processing as one instruction in a high-level language.

(b) Any two of the following features are good answers.
High-level languages use English for command words.
Complex arithmetic can be performed in one instruction.
They have inbuilt functions.
One high-level instruction translates into many machine-code instructions.
The program can be broken down into procedures.

(c) Saves paper by storing data electronically.
Saves space and the need for filing cabinets.
There are dangers from the disposal of computing equipment, which contains toxic materials.
There are fewer jobs, since people can be more productive at a computer.

## ANSWER TO QUESTION 2

(a) A False    B True    C False    D True    E True    F False

(b) (i) A compiler was used because it produces object code, which is not the case with an interpreter.

(ii) The program cannot be edited, because it requires the source code to be edited.
Only the object code is available, which is in machine code, and it would be extremely difficult to edit a machine-code program.

## ANSWER TO QUESTION 1

(a) Machine code

(b) High-level language

# QUESTIONS AND ANSWERS 3

## QUESTION 1

Gwen is a sales manager for a small carpet company. She is using a desktop computer to word-process a report on her department's sales figures.

State whether each of the following activities would increase or decrease Gwen's power consumption.

**(a)** Switching to YouTube to watch a video instead of using the word-processing program.

**(b)** Playing music in the background on the media player.

**(c)** Switching to her laptop computer so that she can work in her room.

Marks 1, 1, 1

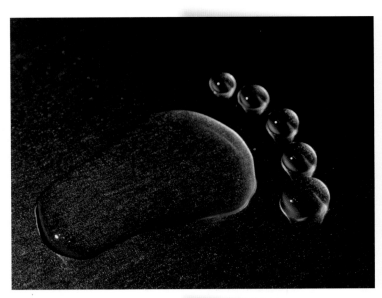

## QUESTION 2

The growth in prevalence of IT equipment has had consequences for the environment.

**(a)** Explain what is meant by the term 'carbon footprint'.

**(b)** Explain how the manufacture and use of computers contributes to the carbon footprint.

**(c)** Apart from the carbon footprint, describe another way in which the growth of computing has a damaging effect on the environment.

Marks 1, 1, 1

## QUESTION 3

Only a few decades ago, screensavers were very popular on desktop and laptop computers. Today they are considered to have a negative impact on the environment.

**(a)** Why is it that screensavers increase the power used by a computer monitor?

**(b)** Modern monitors have settings that allow their power consumption to be reduced.

Describe **two** ways of reducing the power consumption of a monitor.

Marks 1, 2

# QUESTION 4

Sandy has just bought a new computer and is not sure about how to use the power settings.

A friend has told him that he can use the power setting to automatically shut down the computer when he is not using it for more than 5 minutes to reduce its power consumption.

**(a)** Explain why this is not good advice, and describe an alternative course of action for Sandy to take.

**(b)** Suggest a situation where Sandy should shut down his computer.

**Marks 2, 1**

## ANSWER TO QUESTION 2

**(a)** Carbon footprint is a measure of how much carbon dioxide is produced in the making or use of items such as computing devices.

**(b)** Computing equipment uses electricity, which is produced in power stations by burning fossil fuels such as coal and oil. The waste product of this process is the creation of large amounts of carbon dioxide.

**(c)** Out-of-date computers are just thrown away, which pollutes the environment with plastic, glass, steel and toxic chemicals such as mercury, lead and cadmium.

## ANSWER TO QUESTION 4

**(a)** If Sandy sets his computer to power off after just 5 minutes, then he will constantly need to boot up his computer after even a short break. This will itself take power and also means that Sandy will not be able to pick up from where he left off.

A better approach is to set his computer to automatically go to standby mode, which will use very little power but will also allow him to resume quickly from where he left off.

**(b)** Sandy should shut down his computer when he is not going to use it for a lengthy period of time, such as over the weekend or going away on holiday.

## ANSWER TO QUESTION 1

**(a)** Switching to YouTube would increase the power consumption since displaying video data requires a lot of power to constantly change the colour of pixels.

**(b)** Playing music in the background a second task at the same time as the word-processing, which will increase the power use.

**(c)** Switching to her laptop computer will reduce the power since it has a smaller screen which is required to work off its battery and uses less power.

## ANSWER TO QUESTION 3

**(a)** Screensavers are set to be played during periods of inactivity. Power is required to produce the changing images on the screen compared to leaving the screen static or switching it off.

**(b)** The brightness level can be set to an appropriate level for the surrounding light so that it is not using up more power than it needs to.

Settings can be used to make the monitor go automatically into sleep mode when not being used for a specified period of time.

# QUESTIONS AND ANSWERS 4

## QUESTION 1

The last twenty years have seen the introduction of computer networks into schools with internet access. Most schools take steps to manage the activities of their students when they are given access to the internet.

**(a)** Why do most schools install firewalls on their computer network?

**(b)** Which of the following are functions performed by a firewall?

**A** Protecting a network by filtering unwanted data from the internet.

**B** Encrypting network data.

**C** Identifying and removing viruses.

**D** Blocking access to certain internet sites.

**E** Increasing the speed of data transmission.

Marks 1, 2

## QUESTION 2

Allison is the manager of a cat and dog home in Edinburgh. She uses the office network to access other cat and dog websites to research rare breeds and their food requirements.

Allison often finds that some of the sites that she visits are blocked.

**(a)** State the name of the security precaution that is being used at Allison's work, and describe its function.

**(b)** How can Allison get around this problem so that she can access these blocked sites?

Marks 1, 1

## QUESTION 3

Brody works for the security department of a credit-card company where he deals with lost or stolen cards.

When a card is reported lost or stolen, he cancels the card and produces a new one.

**(a)** Brody uses email to communicate with customers about their new credit card. Any documents that contain card details are encrypted.

Explain the term encryption.

**(b)** Apart from financial data, describe another type of data that should be encrypted.

**(c)** If an encrypted file was accessed by a hacker, what would the hacker need to do to view the file?

Marks 1, 1, 1

# QUESTION 4

A security suite is a group of utility programs that protect a computer.

Security suites usually contains a firewall and password protection of the data stored on the computer system.

**(a)** State **two** other items that you would expect to find in a security suite.

**(b)** Explain why password protection of data would be useful in a large family where all the members of the family used the same computer.

Marks 2, 1

## ANSWER TO QUESTION 1

**(a)** Most schools install firewalls to filter traffic to and from the internet so that unsuitable websites are blocked and only to allow trusted users to access the school network.

**(b)** A and D.

## ANSWER TO QUESTION 2

**(a)** The security precaution is a firewall which filters the internet traffic coming in and out of a computer system.

**(b)** Allison can ask the network manager to remove specific websites from the firewall so that they are no longer blocked.

She could access restricted websites on another device such as her tablet or smartphone.

## ANSWER TO QUESTION 3

**(a)** Encryption is the process of protecting data by hiding it using an encryption key to put it into code.

**(b)** Passwords, personal information, national security files and so on.

**(c)** The hacker would need to acquire the correct decoding key to decrypt the file and view it.

## ANSWER TO QUESTION 4

**(a)** Two other items that you would expect to find in a security suite are anti-virus software and spyware/malware/adware removal.

**(b)** Each member of the family would have their own private files.

A security suite would allow each member of the family to set up their own folder that only they can access under password control.

# DATABASE DESIGN AND DEVELOPMENT

## ANALYSIS AND DESIGN

### VIDEO

Watch the clip about databases at www.brightredbooks.net/N5Computing

### WHAT IS A DATABASE?

A **database** is an organised collection of records holding data so that it can be stored and accessed quickly. Before computers, organisations such as banks, schools and supermarkets kept their data on a large number of paper records in filing cabinets. The advantages of keeping data on a computer include speed of retrieval of information, easier amendments to data, less waste of paper and space, and password protection to improve the security of files.

On the other hand, computer databases are liable to attacks from hackers where confidential information can be accessed and even changed. There is also the possibility of files being damaged or deleted by a virus attack.

### FILES, RECORDS AND FIELDS

#### File

A database **file** is an organised collection of records on a particular topic. For example, a sports club may keep a file on its members' details, or a zoo may keep a file on the details of each of their animals.

#### Record

A **record** is the data held on one person or thing: for example, a student record in a school database, or an article record in a supermarket stock file.

#### Field

A **field** is the term given to one item of data in a record: for example, the age field in an employee's record, or the price field in a stock record.

### STAGES OF DEVELOPMENT

The development of a database follows a series of stages in the order shown below:

1. Analysis, 2. Design, 3. Implementation, 4. Testing, 5. Evaluation.

An outline of each stage is given below.

1. **Analysis**: an investigation to determine the functional requirements of the database in terms of the inputs, processes and outputs that are carried out.

2. **Design**: identifying the tables and fields (data types, validation and so on) required to solve the problem and the queries and reports.

3. **Implementation**: a database package is used to convert the design into an actual database.

4. **Testing**: the database is tested with carefully chosen test data to make sure that inputs and validation work correctly and that queries give correct results.

5. **Evaluation**: assessing whether the software is fit for purpose and produces accurate output.

### DON'T FORGET

The records of a database are often described as rows. This is because database records are often displayed in tables where each row is showing the data for one record.

# ANALYSIS

The first stage in developing a database is to identify its functional requirements and the end users of the database.

## End user

It is essential that the user interface is appropriate to the end users of the database. A database that is to be used by expert users will have a user interface which would not be appropriate for beginners or young children.

## Functional requirements

The functional requirements describe the functions that the database will carry out in terms of inputs, processes and outputs.

The data that is to be input into tables, the processing of the data by queries and the output of data in reports must all be identified.

### EXAMPLE:

A hockey club requires to store the details of its players (name, position, date of birth, address, email) and coaches (name, address, telephone number, email, salary) in a database.
The database has to be able to select players who were born in a given year and display the selected player records in an alphabetical list.
The database also has to be able to add a percentage increase to the coaches' salaries and display the names and salaries.

| | |
|---|---|
| Input | Enter the names, positions, date of births, addresses and emails into a player table. |
| | Enter the names, addresses, telephone numbers, emails and salaries into a coach table. |
| Processing | Select players who were born in a year and sort into alphabetical order. |
| | Calculate the new salaries. |
| Output | A report of a list of the players born in a given year. |
| | A report of a list of the coaches and their salaries. |

**DON'T FORGET**

The analysis stage of a database project and the analysis stage of a programming project are basically the same. Both of these projects start with identifying the functional requirements (inputs, processes, outputs) of the software and the type of users who will be using the solution.

# DATA PROTECTION ACT

In the modern world, organisations such as companies, governments, sports clubs and medical centres hold personal data on people in databases and other information systems. The Data Protection Act was introduced to protect the rights of individuals in society against misuse of their data being held on computer systems and networks.

The data subjects are the people whose information is being stored. The data users are the people in the organisation who need to use the data to run the business. For example, in a dental practice, the data subjects would be the patients and the data users would be the dentists and secretaries.

## Requirements of the Data Protection Act

The main requirements of this Act are:

- Information must not be given to other organisations without the consent of the individual.

- The data should be accurate and up to date.

- The data must only be used for limited purposes which are specifically stated.

- The data should be kept secure using passwords and physical security such as locks on doors.

# THINGS TO DO AND THINK ABOUT

Consider a database that you have created in your practical work. Try to identify the inputs, processing and outputs performed by the database.

# MORE DESIGN

## SEARCHING AND SORTING

Two important features of a computerised database are performing searches to quickly access records and sorting the records so that they are arranged in a certain order such as by date of birth, account number and so on.

### Sorting

**Sorting** a database means to arrange the records in order. The records can be put in ascending or descending order of one or more fields.

Shown alongside is a database that has been sorted on two fields. The records have been sorted primarily on the Sex field in ascending order and then on the Age field in descending order.

| Sex | Age | Street | City |
|-----|-----|--------|------|
| F | 24 | 2 North St. | Glasgow |
| F | 21 | 66 Brook St. | Glasgow |
| F | 20 | 23 Hamilton Cres. | Edinburgh |
| F | 20 | 10 High St. | Glasgow |
| F | 19 | 125 Laurel Av. | London |
| F | 19 | 20 Black St. | Glasgow |
| M | 22 | 666 Swan St. | Motherwell |
| M | 20 | 99 Cone Cres. | Helensburgh |
| M | 19 | 33 Perth Rd. | Glasgow |
| M | 17 | 4 Cruise Dr. | Dundee |
| ...... | ...... | ...... | ...... |

## FIELD TYPES

The fields in a database can store different types of information. Some will contain numbers, others will store text, some will be holding a date and so on. Databases allow the designer of the database to specify the field type of each field so that the data can be stored and processed in a particular way.

### Text

A **text field** stores a string of characters.
Examples of a text field are Surname, Town, Colour and so on.

### Numeric

A **numeric field** stores numbers.
Examples of a numeric field are Age, Height, Population and so on.

### Date

A **date field** stores a date.
Examples of a date field are Date of Birth, Return to School Date, M.O.T. Date and so on.

### Time

A **time field** stores a time of day.
Examples of a time field are Start Time, Appointment Time, Closing Time and so on.

### Graphics

A **graphics field** stores an image.
Examples of a graphics field are Student Photo, Company Logo, Country Flag and so on.

contd

## Calculation

A **calculation field** (sometimes called a computed field) is calculated from a formula which uses other fields in the record.

For example, an Average field could be calculated from three other fields called Test 1, Test 2 and Test 3 using the formula = ([Test 1] + [Test 2] + [Test 3]) / 3.

## Link

A **link field** stores a **hyperlink** within the database file or a hyperlink to a document outside the database file.

The link could be to a specific record in the database file, another relevant document, an internet site and so on.

## Object

An **object field** stores a linked or embedded document from another application. Examples of object fields are a graph, sound, spreadsheet document, word-processing document and so on.

## Boolean

A **Boolean field** stores just two values, Yes and No.

Examples of a Boolean field are Subscription Paid, Book Returned, Married and so on.

**DON'T FORGET**

A time field stores a time of day in hours, minutes and seconds, and not the time taken for something to take place. For example, the time taken for an athlete to run the 100 metres would be stored in a numeric field and not a time field.

**ONLINE TEST**

Test yourself on analysis and design online at www.brightredbooks.net/N5Computing

# VALIDATION OF DATA

When designing a database, checks can be put in place to stop the user from entering invalid data.

## Restricted choice

This check limits what the user can enter by restricting their choice to a list of acceptable values.

For example, a zodiac sign could be selected from a list of the twelve zodiac signs.

## Presence check

This check is used to stop important data from being missed out and will not allow a field to be left blank.

For example, a website used to book a train journey would require the destination station to be entered.

## Field lengths

A **field-length check** forces the data which is entered to be a specified number of characters long. For example, a code for an item in a catalogue may be required to be 8 characters long. If the user does not enter the required number of characters, then he/she is given an error message and asked to try again.

## Range checks

A **range check** forces the data which is entered to lie in a certain range of values. For example, a mark in an exam out of 50 must be entered as a number between 0 and 50; or a month entered as a number will only accept values from 1 to 12.

## THINGS TO DO AND THINK ABOUT

Creating a database involves the design of the structure of the records. This involves creating the necessary fields to hold the data and specifying their field types.

The design of the database will have consequences for how the data can be retrieved and sorted.

# EVEN MORE DESIGN

## FLAT FILE AND RELATIONAL DATABASES

A **flat-file database** contains records in only one table of data.

Most companies need to store data in a much more complex way than that performed by a single-table flat-file database. They use a **relational database**, which allows data to be stored in several linked tables.

## LINKED TABLES

### Primary keys and foreign keys

A **primary key** and a **foreign key** are used to make relationships between tables.

The primary key is the field that is used to uniquely identify each record in a table. A table can have only one primary key.

A foreign key contains values that correspond to values in the primary key of another table. For example, in a Flights table for an airport database, each Flight record has a Pilot ID field that corresponds to a record in a Pilots table. The Pilot ID field is a primary key of the Pilot table and a foreign key of the Flights table. When a record is added to the Flights table, a value for the Pilot ID comes from the Pilots table.

This means that all of the fields for the pilot are not stored in each Flight record but are simply a foreign key that links to the fields in the Pilot table.

The entity diagram below illustrates the relationship between the tables.

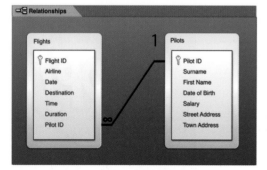

This is an example of a one-to-many relationship. This means that one Pilot ID from the Pilots table will appear in many records in the Flights table. This is a common type of relationship: one author ID will appear in many book records and so on.

### Referential integrity

The value of a primary key in one table has a matching value in the corresponding foreign key of another table.

Referential integrity means that relationships between the tables must always be consistent. Any foreign key must agree with the primary key that it is linked to.

Any changes to a primary key must be applied to all linked foreign keys.

If a Pilot ID was changed in the Pilots table, then any records in the Flights table that have that Pilot ID as a foreign key would also be changed.

## DATA DICTIONARY

A data dictionary is used to illustrate the design of the tables in a database.

It specifies the names and data types of the fields in each table and any validation (length, range, restricted choice, presence check) rules that apply to the data in a field.

The data dictionary also identifies the primary and foreign keys.

Shown below is a data dictionary for a mother-and-child database used by a nursery. The database has two tables called Mother and Child. (The children are all between 3 and 5 years old inclusive.)

contd

**VIDEO**

There are lots of videos on YouTube that explain the basics of database design: enter key words such as 'relational', 'database', 'introduction' and so on.

**Mother Table**

| Attribute | Data Type | Validation | Presence | Key |
|---|---|---|---|---|
| Mother_id | TEXT | Maximum length = 2 | Yes | PK |
| Fullname | TEXT | Maximum length = 12 | Yes | |
| Fees_£ | NUMBER | >= 0 | Yes | |
| Date_of_birth | DATE | Restricted choice | No | |
| Telephone | TEXT | Maximum length = 11 | Yes | |
| Address | TEXT | Maximum length = 40 | Yes | |

**Child Table**

| Child_id | STRING | Maximum length = 2 | Yes | PK |
|---|---|---|---|---|
| Known_as | TEXT | Maximum length = 12 | Yes | |
| Age | NUMBER | >= 2 AND <= 5 | Yes | |
| Sex | TEXT | Max length = 1 | Yes | |
| Allergy | BOOLEAN | Restricted choice (TRUE or FALSE) | No | |
| Mother_id | TEXT | Maximum length = 2 | Yes | FK |

**DON'T FORGET**

A one-to-many relationship between tables is illustrated by using the symbols 1 and ∞.
The ∞ symbol is used in mathematics to represent infinity, but in relational databases it represents many.

**ONLINE TEST**

Test yourself on database structures online at www.brightredbooks.net/N5Computing

## QUERY DESIGN

An important feature of databases is to be able to select data from tables according to search criteria.

It is often useful to sort the selected data on one or more fields to improve the presentation.

Queries are used as a basis of reports which are used to output the information in an attractive layout.

**DON'T FORGET**

The design of a query must specify the search criteria, the fields to be selected and any fields to be sorted. The sort order should be specified as ascending or descending.

**EXAMPLE 1:**

A query is required to display the names of the children who are under 4 years old and the first name, surname and telephone number of their mothers.
The results should be sorted in alphabetical order of the child's name.

**SOLUTION:**

Fields: Child.Known_as, Mother.Fullname, Mother.Telephone
Tables: Child, Mother
Search criteria: Child.Age < 4
Sort order: Child.Known_as Ascending

| Known_As | Fullname | Telephone |
|---|---|---|
| Hamish | Alice Thomson | 07689567329 |
| Megan | Martha Campbell | 07763246819 |
| Paula | Rosaleen Murphy | 07759334890 |
| Sam | Patricia Green | 07890231967 |

## THINGS TO DO AND THINK ABOUT

As part of your practical work for this course, you will be required to create a relational database structure to store information in two tables.

# IMPLEMENTATION, TESTING AND EVALUATION

## IMPLEMENTATION

This will involve the creation of populated tables, queries and reports which match the design.

## SQL (STRUCTURED QUERY LANGUAGE)

SQL stands for Structured Query Language (pronounced 'SQL' or 'sequel').

It is a programming language that is used to manage the data in a relational database.

The examples use the Mother and Child tables shown below.

| Mother | | | | | |
|---|---|---|---|---|---|
| Mother_id | Fullname | Fees_£ | Date_of_birth | Telephone | Address |
| M1 | Susan Macdonald | 560 | 29-Aug-90 | 07752445539 | 22 West Street |
| M2 | Alice Thomson | 970 | 12-Dec-86 | 07689567329 | 36 Hook Avenue |
| M3 | Martha Campbell | 365 | 10-Oct-88 | 07763246819 | 25 Hastings Road |
| M4 | Rosaleen Murphy | 240 | 30-Aug-91 | 07759334890 | 12 South Street |
| M5 | Linda Anderson | 715 | 26-Feb-89 | 07945234078 | 3 New Street |
| M6 | Patricia Green | 490 | 13-Jun-87 | 07890231967 | 19 Shore Road |

| Child | | | | | |
|---|---|---|---|---|---|
| Child_id | Known_as | Age | Sex | Allergy | Mother_id |
| C1 | Carla | 4 | F | FALSE | M1 |
| C2 | Hamish | 3 | M | TRUE | M2 |
| C3 | Megan | 2 | F | FALSE | M3 |
| C4 | Paula | 3 | F | FALSE | M4 |
| C5 | Robert | 5 | M | FALSE | M5 |
| C6 | Sam | 3 | M | FALSE | M6 |
| C7 | Jake | 4 | M | TRUE | M2 |
| C8 | Samantha | 4 | F | TRUE | M6 |

### SELECT statement (FROM, WHERE)

The SELECT statement returns specified fields from a table.

The WHERE keyword is used to select records that meet certain criteria.

**EXAMPLE:**

SELECT Known_as, Age FROM Child WHERE Sex = "F";

| Result | | | | |
|---|---|---|---|---|
| **Known_as** | Carla | Megan | Paula | Samantha |
| **Age** | 4 | 2 | 3 | 4 |

contd

## INSERT

The INSERT statement adds records to a table.

**EXAMPLE:**

INSERT INTO Mother (Mother_id, Fullname, Fees_£, Date_of_birth, Telephone, Address) VALUES ('M7', 'Daphne Higgins', 835, '15-May-80', '07784546523', '103 West Street');

| Mother | | | | | |
|---|---|---|---|---|---|
| M7 | Daphne Higgins | 835 | 15-May-80 | 07784546523 | 103 West Street |

## UPDATE

The UPDATE statement changes data in records that already exist.

**EXAMPLE:**

UPDATE Child SET Known_as = 'Robbie' WHERE Known_as = 'Robert';

| Child | | | | | |
|---|---|---|---|---|---|
| Child_id | Known_as | Age | Sex | Allergy | Mother_id |
| C5 | Robbie | 5 | M | FALSE | M5 |

## DELETE

The DELETE statement removes records from a table.

**EXAMPLE:**

DELETE FROM Child WHERE Age > 4 AND Sex = 'M';

## ORDER BY

The ORDER BY keyword sorts records.

ASC or DESC is used to sort the records in ascending or descending order.

**EXAMPLE:**

SELECT Fullname, Fees_£ FROM Mother ORDER BY Fees_£ ASC;

| Result | | | |
|---|---|---|---|
| **Fullname** | Rosaleen Murphy | Martha Campbell | Patricia Green |
| **Fees_£** | 240 | 365 | 490 |

| | | | |
|---|---|---|---|
| **Fullname** | Susan Macdonald | Linda Anderson | Alice Thomson |
| **Fees_£** | 560 | 715 | 970 |

### Equi-joins between tables

The data from two tables can be combined together using an Equi-Join.

The WHERE clause can be used to select data where a primary key in one table is equal to a foreign key in another table

**EXAMPLE:**

The code below selects the full name of the mother from the Mother table and the child's name from the Child table using the Mother_id as a common field.
SELECT Mother.Fullname, Child.Known_as
FROM Mother, Child
WHERE Mother.Mother_id = Child.Mother_id;

| Result | | | |
|---|---|---|---|
| **Fullname** | Susan Macdonald | Alice Thomson | Martha Campbell | Rosaleen Murphy |
| **Known_as** | Carla | Hamish | Megan | Paula |

| | | | |
|---|---|---|---|
| **Fullname** | Linda Anderson | Patricia Green | Alice Thomson | Patricia Green |
| **Known_as** | Robert | Sam | Jake | Samantha |

## TESTING

The database software should be tested to ensure that SQL operations produce the correct output.

Test data should be chosen, and the expected output should be matched with the actual output to check for errors.

### Accuracy of Output

Queries and reports based on queries should be evaluated for the accuracy of their output. Results of test runs can be used to judge if the database provides accurate output for the functions identified at the analysis stage.

## THINGS TO DO AND THINK ABOUT

The database software that you use in this course will have a feature to write SQL code. Ask your teacher how to explore this feature.

# QUESTIONS AND ANSWERS 1

## INTRODUCTION

The following questions are based on the work of the Database Design and Development area of study. They are intended to be similar to the level and style of questions that you can expect in the exam.

## QUESTION 1

A dog-walking company uses a database to store the details of the dogs that it walks and of their owners. (Some owners have more than one dog.)

The name, sex, breed, age and owner of the dogs as well as the name, address, telephone number and costs for the owners are stored.

When a dog is walked, the charge is added to the fees for the owner, and a printout can be obtained of the owners and their fees.

The database can also be used to provide a list of all of the dogs owned by a specified owner.

**(a)** A database uses reports, tables and queries.

State whether each of these three database items performs input, processing or output.

**(b)** Describe two tables that are required for this database.

**(c)** Describe the input, processing and output requirements of the dog-walking database.

**Marks 3, 2, 3**

## QUESTION 2

Organisations such as banks, companies, sports clubs etc. store personal data about people on computer databases. Legislation exists to give rights to individuals about how this data is stored and used.

**(a)** Name the Act concerned with the storage of personal data on databases.

**(b)** Which of the following activities are covered by the Data Protection Act?

  A   Inaccurate data on an employee must be corrected.

  B   Downloading music from the internet.

  C   Sending a virus in an email attachment.

  D   Printing out the dialogue for *Grease* from a website and selling it on.

  E   Keeping a client database secure with passwords.

  F   Selling customer lists to another company without the customers' consent.

**Marks 1, 3**

## QUESTION 3

Relational databases use a primary and a foreign key to link tables together.

**(a)** Explain how the primary and foreign keys are used to link the tables.

**(b)** A database has a table of film records and a table of film-director records.

Explain why the relationship between the director table and the film table is a one-to-many relationship.

**Marks 1, 1**

## QUESTION 4

A database stores details on subscribers to a social-media website.

One of the records in the database is shown below.

| Name | Alice Hinkly |
|---|---|
| Sex | Female |
| Age | 17 |
| Hobbies | Skiing, Music |
| Star sign | Scorpio |
| House | 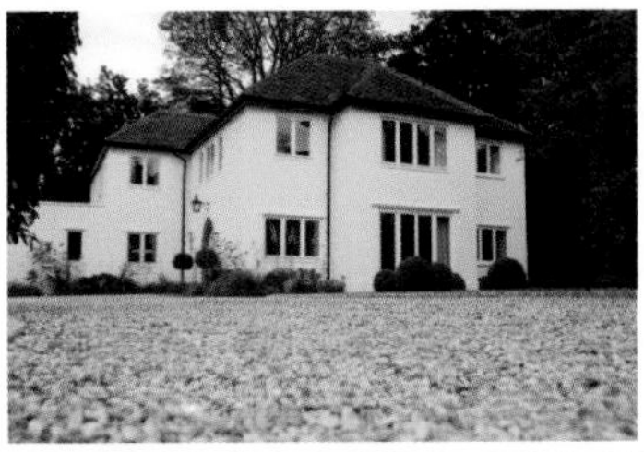 |

**(a)** Describe a type of validation appropriate for the 'Age' field.

**(b)** Describe a type of validation that could be used on the 'Star sign' field.

**Marks 1, 1**

# QUESTIONS AND ANSWERS 2

## QUESTION 1

Mr Strictly works as a teacher in Southton High School. He keeps his student exam marks as a percentage in a database. Ten of the records are shown below.

| Student | Form Class | English | Maths | Science | French |
|---------|-----------|---------|-------|---------|--------|
| Mandy Metcalf | 4C | 66 | 50 | 45 | 35 |
| Zack Greer | 4A | 56 | 70 | 67 | 78 |
| Walter Winters | 4C | 70 | 78 | 88 | 76 |
| Lilly Porter | 4D | 56 | 36 | 41 | 42 |
| Sophie King | 4D | 33 | 67 | 54 | 57 |
| Andrew Green | 4B | 87 | 35 | 66 | 66 |
| Dianna Davidson | 4C | 57 | 51 | 56 | 52 |
| Ronald Aston | 4A | 80 | 68 | 80 | 88 |
| Heather Carson | 4C | 73 | 83 | 75 | 29 |
| Tom Paterson | 4A | 56 | 40 | 55 | 64 |

**(a)** How many fields are there in this database?

**(b)** Name a field that would be suitable for a range check and describe how the range check would operate.

**(c)** Name a field that would be suitable for a length check and describe how the length check would operate.

**(d)** Mr Strictly wants to insert a field to store the average mark for each of the students.

Describe how the database can be used to automatically produce the average marks.

**Marks 1, 2, 2, 2**

## QUESTION 2

A company that sells children's shoes online keeps a relational database of its shoe stock and orders. A stock table and an order table from the database are shown here.

**(a)** Name the primary field in each table.

**(b)** Describe the relationship between the tables indicated by the joining lines.

**(c)** Explain why the Leather Yes/No field in the stock table is a Boolean field.

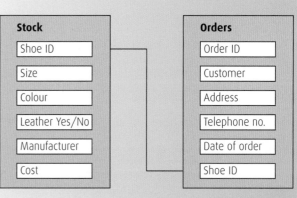

Stock: Shoe ID, Size, Colour, Leather Yes/No, Manufacturer, Cost

Orders: Order ID, Customer, Address, Telephone no., Date of order, Shoe ID

**Marks 2, 2, 1**

# QUESTION 3

Shown alongside is an example of a record from the Orders table in Question 2.

The Orders table is represented in the data dictionary.

State a suitable entry for each of the missing values A to F.

| Field | Data type | Validation | Unique | Key |
|---|---|---|---|---|
| Order ID | INTEGER | >= 1 AND <= 1000 | **A** | **B** |
| Customer | TEXT | Max length = 20 | N | |
| Address | **C** | Maximum length = 30 | Y | |
| Telephone no. | TEXT | **D** | Y | |
| Date of order | DATE | Restricted choice | **E** | |
| Shoe ID | INTEGER | >= 1 AND <= 200 | N | **F** |

**Orders**

| | |
|---|---|
| Order ID | 538 |
| Customer | John Miller |
| Address | 6 North Street, Perth |
| Telephone no. | 07789430024 |
| Date of order | 27/03/2017 |
| Shoe ID | 67 |

**Marks 6**

# QUESTION 4

Shown below is part of a database used to store information about the moons in the solar system.

**(a)** Describe how the data has been sorted.

| Name | Parent planet | Diameter (Km) |
|---|---|---|
| Moon | Earth | 3476 |
| Ganymede | Jupiter | 5276 |
| Callisto | Jupiter | 4820 |
| Io | Jupiter | 3632 |
| Europa | Jupiter | 3126 |
| Triton | Neptune | 4800 |

| Name | Parent planet | Diameter (Km) |
|---|---|---|
| Charon | Pluto | 800 |
| Titan | Saturn | 5140 |
| Rhea | Saturn | 1530 |
| Iapetus | Saturn | 1440 |
| Dione | Saturn | 1120 |
| Tethys | Saturn | 1050 |

**(b)** Name a field that is suitable for restricted choice, and justify your answer.

**Marks 2, 2**

## ANSWER TO QUESTION 4

**(a)** The table has been sorted on the Parent planet field in ascending order and then by the Diameter (Km) field in descending order.

**(b)** The Parent planet field is suitable for restricted choice since the planet can be selected from a limited list (Earth, Jupiter, Neptune, Pluto, Saturn).

## ANSWER TO QUESTION 3

| Field | Data type | Validation | Unique | Key |
|---|---|---|---|---|
| Order ID | INTEGER | >= 1 AND <= 1000 | Y | PK |
| Customer | TEXT | Max length = 20 | N | |
| Address | TEXT | Maximum length = 30 | Y | |
| Telephone no. | TEXT | Maximum length = 11 | Y | |
| Date of order | DATE | Restricted choice | N | |
| Shoe ID | INTEGER | >= 1 AND <= 200 | N | FK |

## ANSWER TO QUESTION 2

**(a)** In the Stock table, the primary field is Shoe ID.

In the Orders table, the primary field is Order ID.

**(b)** This is a one-to-many relationship, since one kind of shoe will appear in many order records. The Shoe ID field in the Stock table is related to many Shoe ID fields in the records of the Order table.

**(c)** The Leather Yes/No field contains only two values, which are Yes and No. A Boolean field is the correct field type for this purpose.

## ANSWER TO QUESTION 1

**(a)** There are 6 fields in the database.

**(b)** The English, Maths, Science or French fields would all be suitable for a range check because they contain data that is a percentage mark. This would mean that any data entered into this field would be validated to be in the range 0 to 100.

**(c)** The Form Class field is suitable for a length check because it contains data that is always two characters long. This would mean that any data entered into this field would be validated to be exactly two characters.

**(d)** A calculated field is inserted into the records, which is a field whose data is automatically calculated from other fields within the record. The formula for the calculated field would be = ([English] + [Maths] + [Science] + [French]) / 4

# QUESTIONS AND ANSWERS 3

## QUESTION 1

A small zoo has a database which keeps details of its animals.

The populated animal table from the database is shown below.

| animal | | | | | |
|---|---|---|---|---|---|
| animal_id | name | species | age | life_expectancy | years_left |
| 1 | Harold | Crocodile | 12 | 45 | 33 |
| 2 | Nellie | Elephant | 56 | 70 | 14 |
| 3 | Huck | Hippopotamus | 41 | 48 | 7 |
| 4 | Samantha | Gorilla | 30 | 32 | 2 |
| 5 | Angel | Parrot | 77 | 110 | 33 |
| 6 | Gwen | Rhinoceros | 25 | 38 | 13 |
| 7 | Lofty | Giraffe | 7 | 11 | 4 |
| 8 | Clarence | Lion | 23 | 35 | 12 |
| 9 | Hoppy | Kangaroo | 4 | 9 | 5 |
| 10 | Barclay | Bear | 5 | 40 | 35 |

**(a)** State which field should be a calculation field, and justify your answer.

**(b)** Design a query to output the name, species and ages of animals that are over 40 years old in ascending order of age.

| name | species | age |
|---|---|---|
| Huck | Hippopotamus | 41 |
| Nellie | Elephant | 56 |
| Angel | Parrot | 77 |

**Marks 2, 2**

## QUESTION 2

A database is used to store data on the Seven Dwarfs.

The populated Dwarfs table from the database is shown below.

| Dwarfs | | | |
|---|---|---|---|
| dwarf_id | name | age | height_cm |
| 1 | Doc | 357 | 125 |
| 2 | Grumpy | 24 | 95 |
| 3 | Bashful | 680 | 115 |
| 4 | Sleepy | 189 | 107 |

| dwarf_id | name | age | height_cm |
|---|---|---|---|
| 5 | Dopey | 262 | 98 |
| 6 | Sneezy | 508 | 122 |
| 7 | Happy | 703 | 116 |

Draw a table to show the results of each of the following SQL instructions.

**(a)** SELECT name, age FROM dwarfs

WHERE age > 120;

**(b)** SELECT name, height_cm FROM dwarfs

WHERE height_cm >= 100 AND height_cm <= 120

ORDER BY height_cm DESC;

**(c)** INSERT INTO dwarfs (dwarf_id, name, age, height_cm)

VALUES (8, 'Slumpy', 172, 103);

**(d)** UPDATE dwarfs SET age = 263 WHERE age = 262;

**(e)** DELETE FROM dwarfs WHERE height_cm > 110;

**Marks 2, 2, 2, 2, 2**

# QUESTION 3

This question uses the Dwarfs table from Question 2.

The Seven Dwarfs do daily chores to run their forest cottage and keep it clean.

The chores are stored in the Chores table shown below.

**Chores**

| task_id | title | done | dwarf_id |
|---------|-------|------|----------|
| 1 | Clean kitchen | Yes | 2 |
| 2 | Cook dinner | No | 4 |
| 3 | Wash dishes | Yes | 6 |
| 4 | Do laundry | No | 5 |
| 5 | Buy groceries | No | 7 |
| 6 | Paint doors | Yes | 1 |
| 7 | Peel potatoes | Yes | 2 |
| 8 | Brush floors | Yes | 4 |
| 9 | Cut grass | No | 3 |
| 10 | Empty bins | Yes | 7 |
| 11 | Clean windows | No | 2 |

**(a)** Draw an entity relationship diagram to show the relationship between the Dwarfs and the Chores tables.

**(b)** Draw a table to show the results of the following equi-joins.

(i) SELECT dwarfs.name, chores.title, chores.done

FROM dwarfs, chores

WHERE dwarfs.dwarfs_id = chores.dwarfs_id;

(ii) SELECT dwarfs.name, chores.title

FROM dwarfs, chores

WHERE dwarfs.dwarfs_id = chores.dwarfs_id AND dwarf_id = 4;

**Marks 2, 4**

---

## ANSWER TO QUESTION 1

**(a)** The years_left field should be a calculation field because it can be found from a formula (= life_expectancy – age).

**(b)** Fields: name, species, age
Tables: animal
Search criteria: age > 40
Sort order: age Ascending

## ANSWER TO QUESTION 2

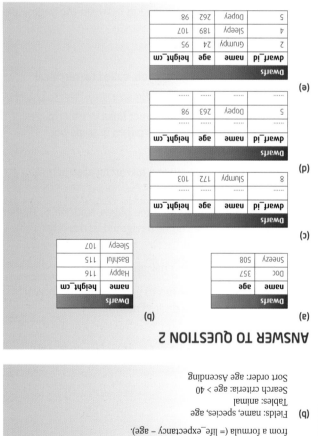

**(a)**

**Dwarfs**

| name | age |
|------|-----|
| Doc | 357 |
| Sneezy | 508 |

**(b)**

**Dwarfs**

| name | height_cm |
|------|-----------|
| Happy | 116 |
| Bashful | 115 |
| Sleepy | 107 |

**(c)**

**Dwarfs**

| dwarf_id | name | age | height_cm |
|----------|------|-----|-----------|
| 8 | Slumpy | 172 | 103 |
| ...... | ...... | ...... | ...... |

**(d)**

**Dwarfs**

| dwarf_id | name | age | height_cm |
|----------|------|-----|-----------|
| 5 | Dopey | 98 | 263 |
| ...... | ...... | ...... | ...... |

**(e)**

**Dwarfs**

| dwarf_id | name | age | height_cm |
|----------|------|-----|-----------|
| 2 | Grumpy | 95 | 24 |
| 4 | Sleepy | 107 | 189 |
| 5 | Dopey | 98 | 262 |

## ANSWER TO QUESTION 3

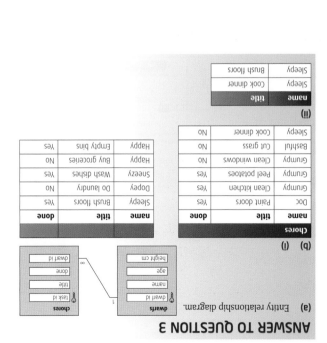

**(a)** Entity relationship diagram.

**(b)** (i)

**Chores**

| name | title | done |
|------|-------|------|
| Doc | Paint doors | Yes |
| Grumpy | Clean kitchen | Yes |
| Grumpy | Peel potatoes | Yes |
| Grumpy | Clean windows | No |
| Bashful | Cut grass | No |
| Sleepy | Cook dinner | No |

| name | title | done |
|------|-------|------|
| Sleepy | Brush floors | Yes |
| Dopey | Do laundry | No |
| Sneezy | Wash dishes | Yes |
| Happy | Buy groceries | No |
| Happy | Empty bins | Yes |

(ii)

| name | title |
|------|-------|
| Sleepy | Cook dinner |
| Sleepy | Brush floors |

# WEB DESIGN AND DEVELOPMENT

## ANALYSIS AND DESIGN

### ANALYSIS

It is important to identify the skills and needs of the end users of the website before development and the functions that it is required to perform.

#### End user

At the analysis stage, it is important to identify the range and types of user who will use the website.

A website that is to be used by pensioners will have a different user interface from an interface that is designed for young children. A children's website would use a small amount of simple text, be colourful and use a lot of images and videos. In general, an adult's website would use more text and be more content-based rather than colourful.

#### Functional requirements

The functional requirements describe what functions the website is required to perform.

For example, the website may be required to create user accounts, display lists of data and images, link to other websites, provide accessibility features for disabled users and so on.

### DESIGN

A website consists of a home page, other pages and usually some external links to other websites.

The design of a website should include a diagram illustrating a plan of the navigation between the pages, and a design of each page.

#### Navigation

There are two types of navigation, called hierarchical navigation and linear navigation.

Hierarchical navigation uses direct links to other pages, whereas linear navigation visits pages in steps one after another.

The 'Exam Revision' site uses a hierarchical structure for navigation.

This means that each of the three pages, National 5, Higher and Advanced Higher, can be navigated to directly from the Exam Revision page.

The 'Flight' site uses linear navigation.

This means that the user has to go through one month after another to get to a desired month.

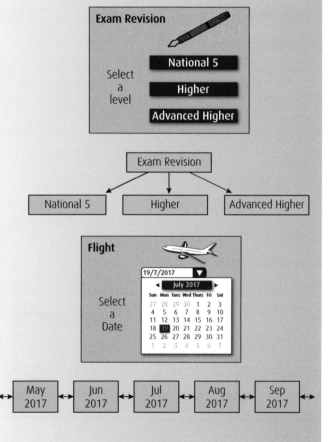

contd

## Wireframe

The wireframe illustrates the design of a webpage for a museum.

It shows the positioning of the elements of the page and the format of files.

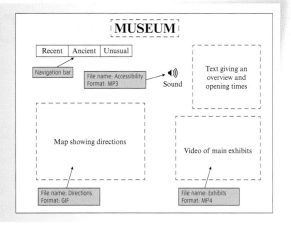

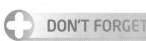
### DON'T FORGET

A wireframe is supposed to be a sketch of the screen interface and not a photographic representation. You should indicate the positioning of elements of the screen such as text, images, video etc. and annotate the sketch with file format information.

# EFFECTIVE USER-INTERFACE DESIGN

The user interface is a term used to describe how the user communicates with a computer. At one time, computing software that was effective in its use was described as 'user-friendly', but this has largely been replaced by the term 'usable'.

## Visual layout

The visual layout refers to the fact that the user interface should be clear, not too cluttered and laid out systematically.

Colour panels can identify different areas of the screen which have a different purpose. Large, bold and coloured text can be used to highlight an important element of the screen.

## Readability

Too much text can take too long to read and can clutter up the screen. For example, hyperlinks should be labelled with simple words and phrases such as Sport, Foreign News, Politics etc.

## Consistency

A good user interface will have a consistent format across multiple pages for menu choices, fonts and the visual display. It easier for the user to learn the package if the interaction with the software is always presented in a similar way.

# COPYRIGHT, DESIGNS AND PATENTS ACT

This law covers the illegal copying of music, films, images, manuscripts and so on.

Over the last decade, there have been rapid technological advances in storage devices and networking which have made it easier to store and transfer unlawful copies of files over the internet. The music and film industries lose billions of pounds each year to piracy.

## Web content (text, graphics, video and audio)

Copyright laws make it illegal to copy text, graphics, video and sound without the owner's permission and then pass it off as your own.

Examples of web content covered by copyright laws include:

| | | | |
|---|---|---|---|
| Text | eBooks, New Articles | Video | Films, YouTube videos |
| Graphics | Photographs, Clipart | Audio | Music, Audio books. |

### ONLINE

Follow the link at www. brightredbooks.net for more information on how copyright laws apply to websites.

# THINGS TO DO AND THINK ABOUT

You will be expected to illustrate the design of computer software for your assignment task with a wireframe. This includes the design of a program interface, a database interface and a web interface.

### ONLINE TEST

Head to www. brightredbooks.net to test yourself on this topic.

# WEB CONTENT AND STANDARD FILE FORMAT

## TEXT, SOUND, GRAPHICS AND VIDEO

Computers are required to store text, sound, graphics and video data. For example, desktop publishing software uses a combination of text and graphics data, and website design uses a combination of text, graphics, video and sound data. The different types of data can be stored in text, graphics, video and sound files which can be imported directly into documents as required.

Most modern websites include image, audio and video content, as well as text, to make the website more attractive and informative for the user.

**ONLINE**

Use the internet to research the technical details of different file formats. Enter the acronyms RTF, GIF, MP3 etc. into a search engine together with keywords such as 'technical', 'description', 'details' etc.

## STANDARD FILE FORMATS

A **standard file format** is a file format that is recognised by other computer programs different from the one that was used to create it. This makes it possible to transfer a file to all programs that recognise the standard format.

For example, if a text document is created in Microsoft Word and then saved as a Word file, then it could not be easily opened by another word-processing program. However, if it is saved in a standard file format for text such as RTF, then other programs can recognise and open the file. The disadvantage is that formatting information such as indents and tables can be lost.

Standard file formats exist for text, sound, graphics and video files. Some examples of standard file formats are described below.

### Audio

**WAV** (Waveform Audio Format) is a file format for sound which uses lossless compression. No quality is lost, but the file sizes are large.

**MP3** stands for layer 3 of the MPEG-1 standard file format. It is a file format that uses lossy compression, so that the quality is reduced. However, techniques such as removing sounds that are inaudible to the human ear can mean that the reduction in quality is barely noticeable. This format is widely used to store music files on computer and portable devices, because typically files are compressed to about one tenth of their size.

**DON'T FORGET**

There are many standard file formats for graphics, but for this course you are only expected to know about JPEG, GIF and PNG. Make sure that you know the difference between them in terms of their types of compression and colour depth.

contd

## Graphics

**JPEG** (Joint Photographic Experts Group) is a file format that uses lossy compression, which means that the quality of the image may be impaired. JPEG uses a bit depth of 24 bits, which provides over 16 million colours.

**GIF** (Graphics Interchange Format) is a file format that uses lossless compression. GIF uses a bit depth of 8 bits, which gives a maximum of 256 colours. Animated GIFs achieve apparent movement by showing a sequence of still frames.

**PNG** (Portable Network Graphics) is a file format for graphics that supports over 16 million colours. PNG can provide lossless compression.

GIF and PNG have a transparency feature that is used to set a colour to transparent which can be useful to remove backgrounds with the same colour from an image.

In the box in the diagram, all of the white pixels have been made transparent.

## Video

Video files are made up of graphics frames that are typically displayed around 20 times per second to create movement. Since video files can be extremely high-capacity, they are normally stored in a compressed file format to reduce their size.

**MPEG** (Motion Picture Experts Group) is a file format that uses lossy compression.

**AVI** (Audio Video Interleave) is an uncompressed file format for video.

## THINGS TO DO AND THINK ABOUT

Standard file formats exist to make it easier to transfer data between different computer programs. There are several other standard formats available for text, sound, graphics and video files, but the key ones are listed in this book.

# FACTORS AFFECTING FILE SIZE

## INTRODUCTION

The quality of graphics, video and sound files is determined by factors such as resolution, colour depth and sampling rate. A computer has a limited amount of storage capacity in main memory and backing store. There is always a balance between improving the quality by increasing the resolution, colour depth and sampling rate and the very large file sizes that result. Compression techniques are used to reduce the size of large multimedia files. **Lossless compression** results in no reduction in quality, but **lossy compression** reduces the quality of the file.

## STORAGE CALCULATIONS

A black-and-white graphic has pixels that can have only two possible states, i.e. black or white. Therefore the colour of each pixel can be stored in 1 bit, with black represented by a 1 and white represented by a 0.

The black-and-white graphic shown here contains 480 × 360 = 172,800 pixels.

Each pixel requires 1 bit of storage.

Total storage requirements = 172,800 bits
= 172,800 / 8 bytes
= 21,600 bytes
= 21,600 / 1,024 Kb
= 21·1 Kb.

## FILE SIZE AND QUALITY

There are several factors that affect the quality of graphics, sound and video files. However, improving the quality has the disadvantage of increasing the file size, since more bits need to be used to store the extra details.

### Resolution

The term **resolution** is a measure of the size of the pixels in an image.

High-resolution graphics have a large number of small pixels.

Low-resolution graphics have a small number of large pixels.

High-resolution graphics have a better quality than low-resolution graphics but have a larger file size since they have to store the colours of more pixels.

The resolution of graphics is usually measured in d.p.i. (dots per inch).

### Colour depth

Bit-mapped graphics use binary codes to represent the colour of each pixel. **Colour depth** is the number of bits that are used for the colour code of each pixel. The higher the number of bits, then the higher the number of colours that can be represented.

Increasing the colour depth will give better-quality colour graphics with a wider range of colours but will also increase the file size.

contd

## Sampling rate

Digital sound is created by taking a sample of a sound many times every second. The **sampling rate** is the number of times that the sound is sampled per second.

A higher sample rate will result in a better-quality digitised sound but will increase the file size, as more sound samples are stored per second. Sampling rates are of the order of many thousands of times per second.

## Frame rate

The quality of video data is determined by the number of frames that are captured per second. Each frame has settings for resolution and colour depth. The file size increases for higher **frame rates**, resolution and colour depth.

# NEED FOR COMPRESSION

Graphic, video and sound files can be very large. These files can be **compressed** to reduce their file size, but they must be decompressed again before they can be used. There are two main advantages of compressing large files on a computer system.

1  Compressed files require less storage space than uncompressed files on storage devices such as hard discs.

2  Compressed files can be transmitted faster over the internet or a computer network, since there is a smaller number of bits to be transferred.

# PROTOTYPES

The end user must be involved early on in the design process to avoid creating a user interface that is not usable and is a waste of time and money.

A prototype is a small-scale version of a website or indeed any software which can be used to get feedback from the end users before committing to the full-scale project.

## Low fidelity

Low-fidelity prototypes are typically paper-based with no coding involved, so they are cheap and can be quickly amended.

A wireframe is an examples of low-fidelity prototyping.

Prototypes of the user interface should be created early on in a project to get feedback from the users and evaluate the suitability of the interface.

 THINGS TO DO AND THINK ABOUT

Look into the settings available for the graphics, video and sound-editing software that you use. Try different settings for resolution, colour depth and so on, and see how they affect the resulting file size.

 DON'T FORGET

Don't confuse sampling rate with sample size. Sample size is the number of bits used to store each sound sample. The higher the sample size, then the better the quality of the sound, since the sample represents the sound with higher definition, but the file size will increase. Typically, sample sizes of 8 bits and 16 bits are used.

 DON'T FORGET

File compression can be either lossy or lossless. Lossy compression reduces the file size but at the expense of detail and quality. Lossless compression uses mathematical techniques to reduce the file size with no loss of detail or quality.

 ONLINE

Find out how file compression works at www.brightredbooks.net/ N5Computing

 ONLINE TEST

Test how well you have learned the factors affecting file size at www. brightredbooks.net/ N5Computing

# HTML 1

## INTRODUCTION

The **World-Wide Web** (WWW) consists of multimedia information stored on the internet on websites.

At one time, websites were created using **Hypertext Mark-up Language** (HTML), but this was very difficult and time-consuming, and these days most websites are created using a web-page editor. Web-page editors allow elements of the website to be dragged and dropped onto the page without the need for writing technically difficult HTML code to achieve the same thing.

## BROWSER

A **browser** is a program that displays web pages and allows the user to navigate around other websites on the internet. Internet Explorer is the most commonly used browser.

Browsers provide other functions such as:

1. Allowing the user to keep a list of shortcuts to favourite websites so that they can quickly be revisited.
2. Keeping a history of recently visited websites.
3. Accessing webmail to send and receive e-mails.
4. The settings can be customised to suit the preferences of the user, for example controlling which toolbars are displayed, which website is initially displayed, the zoom-in/zoom-out factor and so on.
5. Performing the transfer of files over the internet using the File Transfer Protocol (FTP).

**ONLINE**

Go online and download some of the websites that are stored in your favourites. Investigate the component parts of the URL displayed at the top of the screen in the browser.

## URL

Websites can be visited by entering a unique address called a **Uniform Resource Locator** (URL) into a browser program. The URL is made up of several component parts. These parts include the protocol, the domain name, the path to the file and the name of the file.

For example, the URL for a web page about laptops made by Dell on the PC World website is shown below.

http://www.pcworld.co.uk/hardware/laptops/dell.htm

   Protocol    Domain name    Pathway    Filename

The **protocol** is an agreed set of rules between the sender and the receiver that is used to transfer the file. In this case, the Hypertext Transfer Protocol (HTTP) is used to transfer a web page.

**contd**

The **domain name** is the address of the server computer that is hosting the web page. Dots are used to separate the different parts (two or more) of the domain name. The parts are used to specify the type of organisation and the country in which it is based.

The tables alongside show some examples of the parts used in domain names for commonly used organisations and countries.

The pathway specifies the route to the page.

The filename is the name of the actual file that is being accessed.

If the URL is not known for a particular website, then the site and other relevant sites can be found by entering suitable keywords into a **search engine**.

| Part | Meaning |
|------|---------|
| .com | A company |
| .edu | An educational institution |
| .org | A non-profit-making institution |
| .gov | A governmental agency |

| Part | Country |
|------|---------|
| .uk | United Kingdom |
| .fr | France |
| .nz | New Zealand |
| .it | Italy |

## HYPERTEXT MARK-UP LANGUAGE

Hypertext Mark-up Language (HTML) is a language used to create web pages.

It consists of a series of tags which are used to describe the elements of the web page such as a head, title, body, image, audio, hyperlink and so on.

The elements of the page are surrounded by a start tag, <tag>, and a stop tag, </tag>.

### Basic web page

A web page has a head which contains a title and other information and a body which contains the contents of the page. An example of a basic HTML page is shown here.

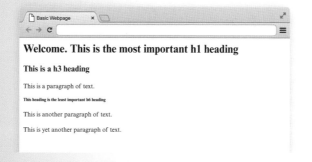

A description of the tags in this code is given below:

- **html**: the <html> tags go around the whole file to specify that it is an HTML file.

- **head**: the <head> tags contain information such as the page title and CSS links (Later!).

- **title**: the <title> tags declare the page title which is displayed in the browser toolbar.

- **body**: the <body> tags go around the main content of the file, which includes elements such as text, images and tables.

- **headings**: headings are defined with the <h1> to <h6> tags.

- <h1> defines the most important heading. <h6> defines the least important heading.

- **paragraph**: paragraphs are defined with the <p> tag. They are used to represent blocks of text that are separated from adjacent blocks.

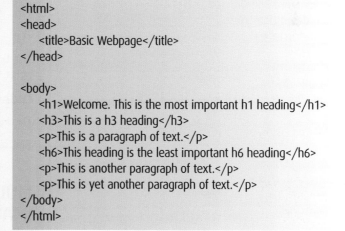

```
<html>
<head>
    <title>Basic Webpage</title>
</head>

<body>
    <h1>Welcome. This is the most important h1 heading</h1>
    <h3>This is a h3 heading</h3>
    <p>This is a paragraph of text.</p>
    <h6>This heading is the least important h6 heading</h6>
    <p>This is another paragraph of text.</p>
    <p>This is yet another paragraph of text.</p>
</body>
</html>
```

 **ONLINE TEST**

Test yourself on HTML at www.brightredbooks.net/N5Computing

 **THINGS TO DO AND THINK ABOUT**

HTML tags can be nested, in the sense that one tag is placed inside another tag. For example, the title tag is nested inside the head tag. Think about other examples of nesting in HTML documents.

# HTML 2

## DIVISIONS

Web pages can be divided up into sections using the <div> tag.

```
<html>
<head>
    <title>Sections</title>
</head>
<body>
    <p>This is a paragraph of text.</p>
    <div style="font-size: 36px;">
        <h3>This is a h3 heading in a div tag.</h3>
        <p>This is a paragraph in the same div tag.</p>
        <p>This is another paragraph in the same div tag.</p>
    </div>
    <p>This is another paragraph of text.</p>
</body>
</html>
```

This example uses the <div> tag to format the font size of a block of code to 36 by setting the style attribute (style="font-size: 36px;").

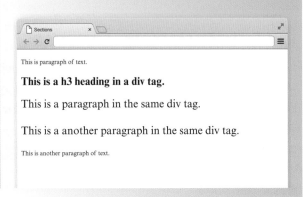

## LISTS WEB PAGE

```
<html>
<head>
    <title>Lists</title>
</head>
<body>
    <h1>Unordered and Ordered Lists</h1>
    <p>Unordered List.</p>
    <ul type="circle">
    <li>Cat</li>
    <li>Hamster</li>
    <li>Rabbit</li>
    <li>Dog</li>
    </ul>
    <p>Ordered List.</p>
    <ol>
    <li>Morning</li>
    <li>Afternoon</li>
    <li>Evening</li>
    <li>Night</li>
    </ol>
</body>
</html>
```

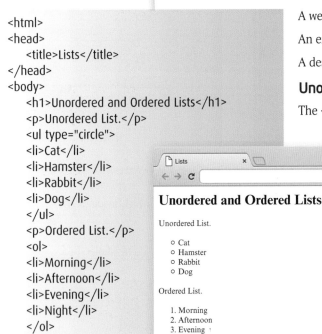

A web page can contain ordered and unordered lists.

An example of lists in an HTML page is shown here.

A description of the list tags in the above code is given below.

### Unordered list

The <ul> tags go around the whole list.

The <li> tags go around each element in the list.

The type attribute is used to specify the type of bullet point that is used.

### Ordered list

The <ol> tags go around the whole list.

The <li> tags go around each element in the list.

## MULTIMEDIA ELEMENTS (TEXT, IMAGES, AUDIO, VIDEO)

Web pages can contain text, image, audio and video media.

An example of a multimedia HTML page is shown here.

A description of the multimedia tags in the above code is given below.

### Image

An image is defined with the <img> tag.

The width and height attributes define the dimensions of the image in pixels.

The src attribute is used to specify the path to the image file.

---

**DON'T FORGET**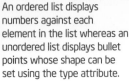

An ordered list displays numbers against each element in the list whereas an unordered list displays bullet points whose shape can be set using the type attribute.

contd

## Audio

Audio is defined with the `<audio>` tag.

The controls, autoplay, loop and src attributes are used as follows;

| | |
|---|---|
| controls | the play, stop, pause, etc. controls are displayed |
| autoplay | the audio file is played automatically when the page is loaded |
| loop | the audio file is repeated in a loop |
| src | the path to the audio file. |

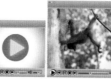 

**Text, Image, Audio and Video**

An orangutan is the most intelligent primate after humans

## Video

Video is defined with the `<video>` tag.

The width, height, controls, autoplay, loop and src attributes are used as follows;

| | |
|---|---|
| width | the width of the video in pixels |
| height | the height of the video in pixels |
| controls | the play, stop, pause, etc. controls are displayed |
| autoplay | the video file is played automatically when the page is loaded |
| loop | the video file is repeated in a loop |
| src | the path to the video file. |

```html
<html>
<head>
    <title>Multimedia</title>
</head>
<body>
    <h1>Text, Image, Audio and Video</h1>
    <p>An orangutan is the most intelligent primate after humans.</p>
    <img width="480" height="360" src="Orangutan.jpg">
    <audio controls autoplay loop src="Call.mp3"></audio>
    <video width="460" height="280" controls>
    <source src="Wildlife.mp4" type="video/mp4">
    </video>
</body>
</html>
```

 **DON'T FORGET**

Audio and video tags both have the attributes of controls, autoplay and loop to manage how the media is played when the page is loaded.

 **DON'T FORGET**

An **absolute hyperlink** refers to the use of the complete URL, e.g. http://www.bbc.co.uk/weather.html. A **relative hyperlink** uses a path from the current directory to the destination page, e.g. sport.html.

# HYPERLINKS (INTERNAL, EXTERNAL)

Hyperlinks specify a link to an URL and the text that is clicked to activate the link.

An internal hyperlink is a link to a webpage or file stored **within the same site**.

An external hyperlink is a link to a webpage or file stored **in another website**.

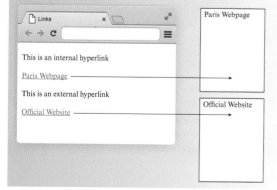

 **ONLINE TEST**

Test yourself on this topic at www.brightredbooks.net

```html
<a href="http://www.bbc.co.uk//">BBC Website</a>
```

```html
<html>
<head>
    <title>Links</title>
</head>
<body>
    <p>This is an internal hyperlink.</p>
    <a href="Paris.html">Paris Webpage</a>
    <p>This is an external hyperlink.</p>
    <a href="https://www.visitparis.fr">Official Website</a>
</body>
</html>
```

 **ONLINE**

Visit the Digital Zone to practise the HTML tags used in this book and to explore more advanced features.

 **THINGS TO DO AND THINK ABOUT**

There are many more HTML tags than the ones used in this course. Research other HTML tags such as `<u>`, `<br>`, `<hr>` etc.

# CSS

## CASCADING STYLE SHEETS (CSS)

HTML is a mark-up language used to specify the content of a web page including paragraphs, headings, images, audio, links, tables etc.

CSS is the language used to describe the formatting and presentation of web pages by specifying fonts, text alignments, colours, backgrounds etc.

## CSS RULES

A CSS rule consists of an identifier (body, h1, p etc.) and a declaration block that contains Properties and their Values.

The property and the value are separated by a colon.

In the example here, the identifier h1 has four properties set to values.

In the example alongside, the identifier body has its background property set to the colour blue.

```
h1
{
font-family: Tahoma, Cambria, Helvetica;
font-size: 16px;
color: blue;
text-align: center;
}
```

```
body
{
background-color: blue;
}
```

## CLASSES AND IDs

Classes and IDs are selectors that define CSS rules which can then be selected by elements such as body, h1, p etc.

### Class example

A class selector is given a name preceded by a full stop ('.').

In this example, the class is called 'myclass' and is selected by the h1 and p elements.

```
<html>
<head>
    <title>Classes</title>
    <style>
        .myclass
        {
        text-align: center;
        color: blue;
        }
    </style>
</head>
<body>
    <h1 class="myclass">This heading is blue and center-aligned</h1>
    <p class="myclass">This paragraph is blue and center-aligned</p>
</body>
</html>
```

```
<html>
<head>
    <title>More Class</title>
    <style>
        p.highlight {
        background: yellow;
        }
    </style>
</head>

<body>
    <p>This text is not highlighted.</p>
    <p class="highlight">This text is highlighted.</p>

    <p>This is more text that is not highlighted.</p>
    <p class="highlight">This is more text that is highlighted.</p>
</body>
</html>
```

| More Class.html | × |

This text is not highlighted.

This text is highlighted.

This is more text that is not highlighted.

This is more text that is highlighted.

| Classes | × |

**This heading is blue and centre-aligned**

This paragraph is blue and centre-aligned

contd

### ID example

An ID selector is given a name preceded by a hash character ('#').

In this example, the ID is called 'myid' and is selected by the first p element.

```html
<html>
<head>
    <title>IDs</title>
    <style>
        #myid
        {
        text-align: center;
        color: white;
        background-color: orange;
        }
    </style>
</head>

<body>
    <p id="myid">This heading is using the ID.</p>
    <p>This paragraph is not using the ID.</p>
</body>
</html>
```

## INTERNAL STYLESHEETS

An internal style sheet is used to define a style for a single HTML page.

The downside of using an internal stylesheet is that changes to the internal stylesheet only affect the page the code is inserted into.

```html
<html>
<head>
    <style>
        body {background-color: hotpink;}
        h1 {color: blue;}
        p {color: green; font-size: 24px;}
        .ptfc {color: yellow; background-color: red; font-size: 72px;}
    </style>
</head>

<body>
    <h1>This is a heading</h1>
    <p>This is a paragraph.</p>
    <p class="ptfc">Go the Jags!</p>
</body>
</html>
```

## EXTERNAL STYLESHEETS

An external style sheet is used to define the style for many HTML pages.

An external style sheet is defined in a separate .CSS file.

A link to the external style sheet is placed in the <head> section of the HTML page.

The look of an entire website can be changed by changing the CSS rules in one file.

```html
<html>
<head>
    <link rel="stylesheet" href="mystyles.css">
</head>

<body>
    <h1>This is a heading</h1>
    <p>This is a paragraph.</p>
    <p class="ptfc">Go the Jags!</p>
    </body>
</html>
```

**External File (mystyles.css)**
```css
body {background-color: hotpink;}

h1 {color: blue;}

p {color: green; font-size: 24px;}

.ptfc
{color: yellow;
background-color: red;
font-size: 72px;
}
```

 **VIDEO LINK**

Go to YouTube and search for "CSS Tutorial for Beginners 01" for a video lesson on CSS.
The first 10 videos in this series cover the basics and some extras.

 **ONLINE TEST**

Test yourself on this topic at www.brightredbooks.net

 **THINGS TO DO AND THINK ABOUT**

Use the code in this spread to create your own style sheets.

Try out the external as well as the internal style sheets.

# JAVASCRIPT

## INTRODUCTION

JavaScript is a programming language that can be incorporated into HTML pages. It is a scripting language and therefore cannot be used to create stand-alone programs. JavaScript is used to add interactivity to web pages and make them more dynamic. For example, JavaScript can be used to validate data that is entered into forms, give warning and confirmation messages to the user and provide information on the system date and time. Command buttons, check boxes, radio buttons and other controls can be added to web pages to provide added functionality.

```
<html>
    <head>
        <title>
            Christmas Countdown
        </title>
        <script type="text/javascript">
        </script>
    </head>
    <body>
        <script>
            var y=window.prompt("Please enter your name.")
            document.write("Hello "+y+", welcome to my website.");
            //Set the two dates
            today=new Date()
            var christmas=new Date(today.getFullYear(), 11, 25)
            if (today.getMonth()==11 && today.getDate()>25) //if Christmas has passed
            christmas.setFullYear(christmas.getFullYear()+1) //calculate for next year
            //Set 1 day in milliseconds
            var one_day=1000*60*60*24
            //Calculate the difference between the two dates and convert to days
            document.write(" There are "+Math.ceil((christmas.getTime()-
            today.getTime())/(one_day))+" days left until Christmas!")
        </script>
    </body>
</html>
```

**Christmas Countdown**

Hello Tom, welcome to my website. There are 159 days left until Christmas!

The example shown here asks the user to enter their name and then gives a personal welcome followed by a message stating how many days are left until Christmas.

The tags <script type="text/javascript"> and </script> are placed in the <head> section to declare the scripting language being used.

The actual JavaScript code is placed in the <body> section surrounded by the <script> and </script> tags.

```
<html>
<head>
    <title>Contact</title>
</head>

<body>
    <h2>Contact Us</h2>
    <button onclick="contact()">Contact number</button>
    <script>
        function contact() {
        alert("Call 07785 567128 for our helpline.")
        }
    </script>
</body>
</html>
```

**Contact**

**Contact Us**

Contact number

This page says:
Call 07785 567128 for our helpline.
OK

The code shown here creates a button which executes a JavaScript function called contact when it is clicked.

The function uses an alert box to give a contact telephone number.

# ONMOUSEOVER AND ONMOUSEOUT

Mouse events are where code is executed whenever the mouse performs an action such as moving over an image or moving out of a heading.

The following example uses two functions called bigGrumpy() and smallGrumpy() which are run when the mouse pointer moves over and when the mouse pointer moves away from an image of a dog called Grumpy.

The bigGrumpy function enlarges the size of the image and the smallGrumpy function reduces the size of the image.

**DON'T FORGET**

JavaScript is a very complex language with lots of features and functions. As far as this course is concerned, you should need to be able to describe and identify the use of the Onmouseover and Onmouseout mouse events.

```html
<html>

<head>
    <title>Mouseover and Mouseout</title>
</head>

<body>
    <h1>Move the mouse pointer over Grumpy the dog.</h1>
    <img onmouseover="bigGrumpy(this)" onmouseout="smallGrumpy(this)"
src="Grumpy.bmp">
    <p>Change Grumpy's size.</p>

    <script>
        function bigGrumpy(x) {
        x.style.height = "300px";
        x.style.width = "240px";
        }

        function smallGrumpy(x) {
        x.style.height = "125px";
        x.style.width = "100px";
        }
    </script>
</body>
</html>
```

The following example uses the onmouseover and onmouseout mouse events to change the colour of an h1 heading when the mouse pointer moves over the heading.

```html
<html>

<head>
    <title>Heading Colour Change</title>
</head>

<body>
<h1 onmouseover="style.color='red'" onmouseout="style.color='black'">Mouse
over this text</h1>
</body>
</html>
```

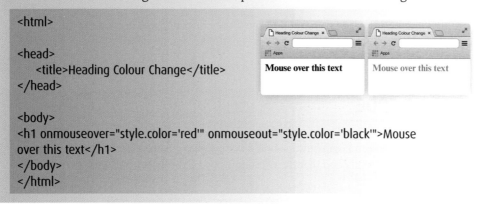

**ONLINE**

Follow the link at www.brightredbooks.net for a practical example of the onmouseover event. There is also an onmouseout example on the same site.

## THINGS TO DO AND THINK ABOUT

You can try out JavaScript by entering code into a simple text editor such as Notepad. Try out the examples in this spread; but you will need to create a cat image for the Onmouseover and Onmouseout example which should be placed in the same folder as the code file.

# TESTING AND EVALUATION

## THE NEED FOR TESTING

Once a website has been analysed, designed and implemented, then it should be thoroughly tested to detect and remove any errors.

Testing a website covers several areas including checking that the solution matches the design, ensuring that all links work, checking that media files play correctly and checking that code is free from errors.

## CHECK THAT THE IMPLEMENTATION MATCHES THE USER INTERFACE DESIGN

Once the website has been developed, checks must be made to ensure that the implementation matches the design.

For example:

- A check that spelling and grammar are accurate.
- A check that the elements of the page (text, graphics, video, navigation bars and so on) are positioned in the same way as in the wireframe design.

## LINKS AND NAVIGATION

Websites contain internal hyperlinks to pages within the same website, external hyperlinks to other websites and links to data files.

All of the links and the navigation systems should be tested to see if they work properly.

**DON'T FORGET**

Testing a website is similar to testing a program to make sure the code is correct, but it also includes wider aspects of testing such as checking hyperlinks and media files to see if they operate properly.

**DON'T FORGET**

Links can be internal or external. Make sure that internal links have the correct relative/absolute address and that the paths to external website are all directed to valid URLs.

## MEDIA (TEXT, GRAPHICS, VIDEO, AUDIO) DISPLAY CORRECTLY

Text and graphics should be checked to see if they display correctly without being cropped or difficult to make out. Video and audio files should be run to see if they play properly and that the quality is good.

## TESTING CODE

Websites also contain JavaScript and other code to add interactivity and to provide dynamic content. For example, a Login button should be tested to ensure that the script associated with it executes correctly and that the username and password are validated correctly.

# TESTING FOR CONSISTENCY

Navigation bars, font formatting, image sizes, background colours etc. should be checked across all of the website pages for consistency of appearance.

For example, it is poor consistency to use different fonts and font sizes for the captions used for a list of images.

> **EXAMPLE:**
>
> The Vodafone website shown below provides a navigation bar to navigate to the main sections of the website (Shop, Broadband, Explore, My Vodafone and Support).
> There are also 'Learn more' and 'Pre-order now' links.
> The home page contains a store finder, coverage checker and allows existing customers to log into their account.

There is also a search box for users of the website to enter keywords to return results.

Testing this website when it was being developed would involve the following:

- checking that the screen matches the user interface design

- ensuring that the correct elements are on each page and laid out correctly

- checking that the spelling and grammar are correct

- checking that the navigation bar leads to the correct pages within the website for Shop, Broadband, Explore etc.

- checking that the internal hyperlinks lead to the correct web page for 'Learn more' and 'Pre-order now'.

- checking that images, audio and video all display and run properly

- checking that the code for the Find a store, Coverage checker and Log in functions execute correctly

- checking that font formatting, colours, menus etc. are consistent throughout the website.

# EVALUATION

Finally, the website should be evaluated to see if it is fit for purpose.

Both the functionality and the user interface of the website should be assessed to see if the requirements are delivered and if the interface is suitable for the end users.

For example, a website that is intended for older users should not have an interface with very small text that would be hard for them to read.

 **THINGS TO DO AND THINK ABOUT**

Look at a website that you have created as part of this course.

Think about how you would apply the concepts outlined in this spread to test it.

Does it match your original design? Do all of the hyperlinks work properly? Do image/audio/video files work properly? Are the different pages consistent? Does the code give the expected output from test data?

**ONLINE**

Visit the Digital Zone for more information on testing websites.

 **ONLINE TEST**

Test yourself on this topic at www.brightredbooks.net

# QUESTIONS AND ANSWERS 1

## QUESTION 1

Computers are used by experienced and highly technical users but also by young and inexperienced users.

**(a)** Why do software packages that have a user interface with icons and pull-down menus also provide keyboard shortcuts?

**(b)** Tablet computers use a touchscreen for user input. Describe an advantage and a disadvantage of this type of input compared to a keyboard and mouse.

**(c)** Describe two ways in which the user interface can be designed to make it suitable for a disabled user.

Marks 2, 2, 2

## QUESTION 2

Kyle has created a photograph for the school website on his home computer using a graphics program that is different from the one that he uses at school.

The school computer will not open the graphic file that he created on his home computer.

**(a)** Explain how a standard file format can solve this problem.

**(b)** Name two possible standard file formats that Kyle could use.

**(c)** State which of the two file formats would be more suitable, and give a reason for your answer.

Marks 1, 2, 2

## QUESTION 3

A company called Party Fun sells and hires out fancy-dress costumes, masks and tricks on their website. The URL for a web page displaying celebrity masks is shown below.

http://www.partyfun.co.uk/masks/celebrities.htm

    A       B       C       D

Describe the component parts A, B, C and D of the URL.

Marks 4

## QUESTION 4

Wendy is a student in Graymore High School. She has been asked to create two black-and-white bit-mapped graphics for her Art coursework.

**(a)** Calculate the storage requirement of each graphic in kilobytes.

    (i)    480 pixels

    600 pixels

    (ii)    1,800 pixels

    960 pixels

**(b)** Wendy creates a high-resolution and high-bit-depth graphic for the front cover of the program for the school sports. She saves the file and notices that it has a high capacity of 6·2 Mb.
Describe two ways in which she can reduce the file size without cropping or changing the size of the image.

**Marks 4, 2**

---

### ANSWER TO QUESTION 4

**(a)** (i) The image contains 480 × 600 = 288,000 pixels.
Each pixel requires 1 bit of storage.
Storage requirements = 288,000 bits = 288,000 / 8 bytes = 36,000 bytes
= 36,000 / 1,024 Kb
= 35·2 Kb.

(ii) The image contains 1,800 × 960 = 1,728,000 pixels.
Each pixel requires 1 bit of storage.
Storage requirements = 1,728,000 bits = 1,728,000 / 8 bytes
= 216,000 bytes
= 216,000 / 1,024 Kb
= 210·9 Kb.

**(b)** Wendy could save the file in a lower resolution or reduce the number of colours by lowering the bit depth.

---

### ANSWER TO QUESTION 3

**A** The protocol (Hypertext Transfer Protocol) used to transfer the web page.

**B** The domain name, which is the address of the server computer that is hosting the web page.

**C** The pathway or route to the page.

**D** The filename of the file that is being accessed.

---

### ANSWER TO QUESTION 2

**(a)** Kyle could save the file in a standard file format for graphics which would be opened by most graphics programs.

**(b)** JPEG, GIF, PNG and so on.

**(c)** PNG would be the most suitable because it supports over 16 million colours and uses lossless compression.
GIF has a smaller colour depth than PNG.
JPEG uses lossy compression, so quality will be lost.

---

### ANSWER TO QUESTION 1

**(a)** Using icons and pull-down menus is easy to use for novice users who can explore the menus with the mouse pointer. However, an experienced user can find this kind of interface slow and clumsy and would prefer to use keyboard shortcuts which he/she can enter more quickly and more efficiently.

**(b)** Touchscreens save space by replacing the physical keyboard with a pop-up keyboard that appears on the screen; however, most people would find it slower to enter data compared to a traditional keyboard and mouse.

**(c)** Voice recognition can be used for people who do not have the use of their limbs.
Icons and the font size of text in menus can be made larger for people with poor eyesight.

# QUESTIONS AND ANSWERS 2

## QUESTION 1

Sam is creating a website for his new online furniture business.

He copies some images of tables and chairs from other leading furniture companies' websites to put on his home page to make it look more attractive.

**(a)** Name the law that makes what Sam is doing illegal.

**(b)** Describe two other internet activities that would be made illegal by this law.

Marks 1, 2

## QUESTION 2

**(a)** The design of a web page for a city bus tours company is shown here.

What name is given to the type of diagram shown here to illustrate the design of a web page?

**(b)** Describe two advantages of using this diagram at the design stage.

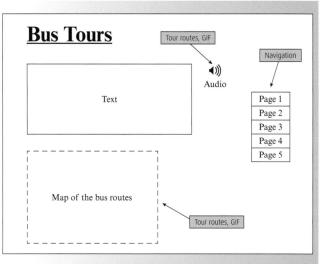

Marks 1, 2

## QUESTION 3

**(a)** Describe two features of HTML code.

**(b)** Shown below is HTML code for the homepage of a 'Doughnut' website. There are three errors in the code.

Write out the line number of each error and the corrected code.

```
Line 1      <html>
Line 2      <head>
Line 3          <title>Doughnut World</title>
Line 4      <head>
Line 5      <body>
Line 6          <h1>Welcome to Doughnut World </h1>
Line 7          <p>We have the tastiest doughnuts on the planet</p>
Line 8          <h3>Menu</h4>
Line 9          <p>Plain doughnuts</p>
Line 10         <p>Iced doughnuts</p>
Line 11         <p>Cream doughnuts</p>
Line 12         <p>Chocolate doughnuts</p>
Line 13     </body
Line 14     </html>
```

Marks 2, 3

## QUESTION 4

The 'Scotland's got Talent' website has a home page which has images and video files of contestants' performances.

**(a)** Complete the HTML code below to display an image named 'kangaroodance.png' with a width of 400 pixels and height of 320 pixels.

<img ................................................. src ...........................................................>

**(b)** A video file named 'handskipping.mp4' is to be inserted in a frame with width of 600 pixels and height of 400 pixels.

The video should play automatically when the page is loaded and then continuously repeat itself.

Write code to play the video file.

**Marks 2, 2**

---

## ANSWER TO QUESTION 4

**(a)** `<img width="400" height="320" src="kangaroodance.png">`

**(b)** `<video width="600" height="400" autoplay loop>`
`<source src="handskipping.mp4" type="video/mp4">`

---

## ANSWER TO QUESTION 3

**(a)** HTML code starts with an <html> tag and ends with an </html> tag.

HTML code is made up of tags which define the elements of the web page.

HTML code has a head tag which defines the title of the document, scripts, styles etc.

HTML code has a body tag which defines the content of the web page.

**(b)**

| Line 4 | </head> | (The forward slash was missing in the closing tag.) |
| Line 8 | <h3>Menu</h3> | (The headings are different in the opening and closing tags.) |
| Line 13 | </body> | (The body tag had no closing bracket.) |

---

## ANSWER TO QUESTION 2

**(a)** A wireframe.

**(b)** The relative positioning of text, images, videos, hyperlinks etc.

The file formats of media files (text, graphics, video and audio).

---

## ANSWER TO QUESTION 1

**(a)** Copyright, Designs and Patents Act 1988.

**(b)** Copying multimedia files from a website and using them as your own without the owner's permission.

Downloading music/films/audio books for your own personal use and selling them on.

# QUESTIONS AND ANSWERS 3

## QUESTION 1

HTML and JavaScript are both used in the creation of websites.

A website is required to enter the date of birth of the user and then display their star sign (Aquarius, Pisces, Aries etc.) in text.

**(a)** Explain why JavaScript is required in addition to HTML to perform this function.

**(b)** When the user moves the mouse pointer over the text for the star sign, it displays an image of the sign which disappears when the pointer is moved away.

Name two JavaScript mouse events that have been used in this web page.

**Marks 2, 2**

## QUESTION 2

The CSS rule for the p identifier shown below has **three** errors.

**(a)** Rewrite the rule with the errors corrected.

```
p
{
font-family: Arial, Helvetica, Times New Roman;
font-size: 12px
color blue;
text-align: left;
```

**(b)** Why are three fonts listed and not just one?

**Marks 3, 1**

**DON'T FORGET**

Some questions ask you to give advantages and/or disadvantages in a given situation. There will be obvious answers that the examiner is looking for, but other answers can be accepted. Marking schemes cannot give a limitless number of advantages and disadvantages. Ask your teacher if you are not sure of your answer.

## QUESTION 3

**(a)** What is the difference between internal CSS and external CSS?

**(b)** In which section of a web page is an external link to a CSS file placed?

**(c)** A web page has a link to an external CSS file named 'cool.css'.

Write down the missing values for A, B and C for a link to a CSS file named 'cool.css'.

```
<head>
    <link rel="A" B="C">
</head>
```

**Marks 2, 1, 3**

# QUESTION 4

The Bright Red Publishing website shown here has a navigation bar and hyperlinks to allow the user to navigate to the other pages in the website.

Visitors to the site can register an account/ Log in and search for books.

**(a)** During the development of this website, a check was carried out to make sure that the screen matched the original design.

Describe two checks that should have been carried out.

**(b)** Apart from the screen design, describe two other checks that should have taken place when this website was being developed.

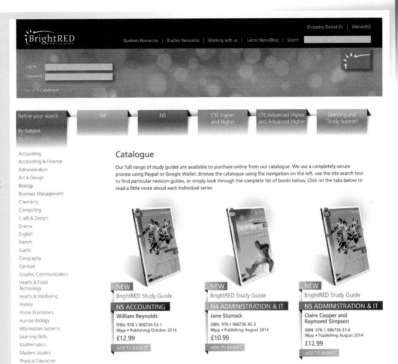

**Marks 2, 2**

---

87

## ANSWER TO QUESTION 1

**(a)** HTML uses tags to create a description of the web page by identifying elements on the page such as a header, title, body, style, font size, image, hyperlinks and so on. However, JavaScript is a scripting language that is used to provide the code that processes the date of birth of the user and then displays the star sign.

**(b)** Onmouseover, Onmouseout.

## ANSWER TO QUESTION 2

**(a)** The corrected rule is given below.

There was a missing semicolon after font-size:12px.
There was a missing colon between color and blue.
There was a missing closing curly bracket at the end of the rule.

```
p
{
font-family: Arial, Helvetica, Times New Roman;
font-size: 12px;
color: blue;
text-align: left;
}
```

**(b)** If the first font in the list is not installed on the device, then the second font is used and so on.

## ANSWER TO QUESTION 3

**(a)** An internal style sheet defines the CSS rules in the <head> section of a page whereas an external style sheet is defined in a separate file.

**(b)** The link is placed in the <head> section of the page.

**(c)**
```
<head>
<link rel="stylesheet" href="cool.css">
</head>
```

## ANSWER TO QUESTION 4

**(a)** A check to make sure that text, hyperlinks, images, video, navigation bars etc. have been placed on the page according to the wireframe design.

A check that spelling and grammar are correct.

**(b)** There are many answers to this question. The most important ones are given below.

Internal and external hyperlinks should be tested to see if they link to the correct location.

Text and images should be checked to see if they display properly.

Audio and video files should be tested to see if they play properly.

The different pages of the website should be checked for consistency in formatting and positioning of the various elements.

Scripts for registering/logging in, searching and so on should be tested to see if they run correctly.

# COURSE ASSESSMENT

## THE COURSE ASSIGNMENT

### INTRODUCTION

The course assessment consists of a practical assignment and an exam paper. The practical assignment is allocated 50 marks out of a total of 160 for the course assessment. Therefore the practical coursework makes up roughly 31% of the total marks for this course – and a good mark here can go a long way towards overall success.

### THE ASSIGNMENT

The assignment is set by the SQA on an annual basis and sent off to be externally marked.

It is made up of three separate tasks.

The marks are allocated across three areas of study which are covered by the assignment as follows:

- Software design and development        (25 marks)
- Database design and development        (10–15 marks)
- Web design and development        (10–15 marks)

The marks are also spread across five development skills as follows:

- Analysis        (5 marks)
- Design        (5 marks)
- Implementation        (30 marks)
- Testing        (5 marks)
- Evaluation        (5 marks)

The purpose of the assignment is to assess your ability to produce a solution to an appropriate computing problem that is based upon the knowledge and skills that you have developed in the two mandatory units. It is set by the SQA and carried out under controlled conditions. This is an open-book assessment, which means that you can look over programs and information systems that you have previously written to refresh your memory on particular skills that you may have forgotten. You can use manuals and textbooks to get more information and extend your skills.

Your teacher is allowed to give you some hints and advice – but do not expect him/her to do the assignment for you. You are expected to show your own initiative in this task and to persevere with a problem in the search for a solution. If your teacher gives you significant support with a particular stage of the problem, then he/she will deduct marks for that stage. On the other hand, don't be frightened of asking your teacher for some help if you are completely stuck. At worst, you will lose a mark or two for one part of your solutions, but it will allow you to progress to the next stage, where you can still gain full marks.

The assignment is not just about finding a practical solution at the computer. It involves analysing a problem, designing a solution, implementing the solution and then testing the solution. You should have picked up the necessary skills to address these stages from the work that you have carried out in the unit assessments. The assignment will give guidance in the form of questions, tasks and prompts that will guide you in clear stages through the assessment.

### ONLINE

You can find lots more details on course assessment for National 5 courses from the Scottish Qualifications Authority website at www.brightredbooks.net/N5Computing

### DON'T FORGET

The course assessment will test your knowledge across both units of the National 5 Computing Science course. If you are unsure of any points, then revise the relevant section in this study guide or ask your teacher for clarification.

# THE REPORT

A word-processed report on the analysis, design, implementation and testing must be provided. Make sure that the report is clear, well presented and free from silly mistakes and spelling and grammatical errors. Have a cover page and appropriate headings and subheadings with consistency in the formatting. Page numbers and headers should be inserted, together with an index page. Avoid using multiple fonts and styles, which would make the document appear cluttered and too 'busy'.

People are impressed by appearances, so don't let your good practical work down by handing in a messy report that is difficult to read.

## Marking the report

The assessment is marked externally by a computing science teacher in another school according to a strict marking scheme provided by the SQA. This is to make sure that there is a consistency of marking across different schools.

## Evidence

You are expected to provide hard-copy evidence for your coursework assignment.

All evidence of your assignment must be submitted to SQA in a paper-based format. This will include your report as well as other evidence such as hard copies of program listings, screenshots of test runs, printouts of web pages and so on.

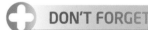

## DON'T FORGET

Remember: the assignment is not assessed on the practical work that you do on the computer alone. The practical implementation is worth 60% of the marks. Make sure that you put the same effort into your analysis, design, testing etc. as you do into the implemented solution.

## THINGS TO DO AND THINK ABOUT

Take time over your assignment, and make sure that the report is complete and clearly presented. Don't hand in your solution until you are sure that it is completely finished. Your teacher is not allowed to return your assignment for further improvement.

# THE EXAM

## INTRODUCTION

The course assessment consists of an exam and a practical assignment. The exam is allocated 110 marks out of a total of 160 for the course assessment. Therefore the exam makes up 69% of the total marks for this course. The exam covers the four mandatory areas, listed below.

The exam is set and marked by the SQA and is sat in centres under the exam conditions specified by the SQA.

## THE QUESTION PAPER

The marks in the exam are distributed across all four areas of study in the percentages shown below:

- Software design and development      (approximately 40%)
- Computer systems                            (approximately 10%)
- Database design and development      (approximately 25%)
- Web design and development              (approximately 25%)

There are two sections in the question paper. You are required to answer all the questions in both sections.

### Section 1      25 marks

This section has short-answer questions that test your knowledge and understanding of the topics listed in the syllabus across the four areas of the course.

### Section 2      85 marks

This section has extended-response questions that test your ability to apply your knowledge and understanding in a challenging problem-solving context from across the four areas of the course.

Total          110 marks

The time allocation for the exam is 2 hours.

### Pace yourself

The exam has 110 marks that have to be done in 120 minutes, so on average you have 1 minute to do each question and 10 minutes at the end to check over your answers. Use this to pace yourself. You want to strike a good balance between finishing the exam in half the time and running out of time halfway

through the paper. Finishing the exam in half the time usually means that you have not given fully explained and detailed answers. You should be finishing Section 1 in a little under 20 minutes. Try to leave yourself enough time at the end of the exam to check over your answers.

# PREPARATION

There is a specimen paper provided by the SQA to give teachers and students an idea of the kinds of questions that they can expect to meet in the actual exam. Your teacher should be able to give you a copy of this paper, or you can download it from the SQA website. It is good preparation to work through this paper, as it will give you a feel for the exam. Also, there are worked answers provided that will give you a good idea of how you are expected to answer the questions.

This, along with past exam papers, will be an invaluable source of revision and will allow you to recognise patterns of questions and topics that come up most frequently. This will allow you to target your revision and improve your chances of success.

You should see this book as an excellent way of consolidating the theory topics covered in class. If you thoroughly learn the contents of this book, then you will have a strong foundation from which to tackle the exam. Remember that you can also use the online Bright Red Digital Zone for extra preparation. Your teacher is also a valuable resource for guidance and preparation. He/she can be a source of extra questions and revision materials or can at least provide information on where to get them for yourself.

## THINGS TO DO AND THINK ABOUT

The exam should not come as a surprise to you. If you have carefully studied the contents of this book, then you should have the knowledge required for section 1 and a good foundation to apply the knowledge in the more challenging questions in section 2. Good luck!

**ONLINE**

The exam timetable is published months before the exams take place in the summer. You can download your own personalised exam timetable from the SQA website.

**DON'T FORGET**

Past exam papers are an excellent resource for revision. However, the content of this course was significantly changed in the session 2017-18, and so some topics in exam papers set before 2018 are no longer part of the course, and some new topics are not covered. Your teacher should be able to help you with which questions you should do.

**ONLINE**

A great way to revise is to use past papers. You can download these for Computing Science and other subjects online. Follow the link at www.brightredbooks.net/N5Computing

# GUIDANCE AND ADVICE

## INTRODUCTION

This section is here to give you some tips on how you can improve your performance in the practical assignment and the exam. Each of these elements is very important, since they contribute 31% and 69% of the total marks respectively. Remember that it is your performance in the course assessment that provides your final grade.

## READ THE FRONT PAGE

The instructions on the front page of the exam paper give you important information on how to answer the questions. This is the same as the information on the front of the specimen question paper. Save yourself some time in the exam by making sure that you know these instructions before you enter the exam room.

**DON'T FORGET**

The marking scheme in the exam gives the number of marks awarded to each question. In general, you should make 1 point for 1 mark, 2 points for 2 marks and so on.

## COMMON MISTAKES

It is a mistake made frequently by students to give answers that are too brief and do not give enough explanation or detail.

The example below illustrates this point by giving a good answer and a bad answer to the same question.

### EXAMPLE:

**Question**

The graphic shown below was created with a vector graphics package. Describe how this image is stored by the program.

**Good answer**

> The image in a vector graphics program is stored as a group of objects together with the attributes of each object. This image would use a rectangle, circle and line object with attributes such as centre x-coordinate, centre y-coordinate, length, breadth, radius, fill colour and so on to describe each shape.

This answer is good because it mentions that vector graphics are stored as objects and attributes and then mentions the actual shapes used in this particular image.

**contd**

## Bad answer

> Different shapes.

This answer gives a hint of what is meant by vector graphics by using the word 'shapes' as opposed to 'pixels' but is far too brief and is not using the appropriate technical terms. Also, there is no description of how vector graphics would store the actual image shown here.

It would have been better to use the word 'objects' rather than 'shapes'. There is no mention that the attributes or features of each object are stored.

It is surprisingly frequent for students to answer their own version of a question rather than the one given in the question paper. This is usually due to not reading the information at the start of the question and then skimming through what is being asked.

Make sure that you read the question properly.

**DON'T FORGET**

It is always a good idea to put any relevant technical terms into your answers. For example, when describing 'bit-mapped', it is better to use the terms 'pixel' and 'resolution' as opposed to 'dots' and 'detail'.

## OUTSIDE THE CLASS

The practical assignment is done under supervised conditions in the classroom. However, there is no problem with you doing preparation work at home. Once you have been given the instructions for the assessment, you should think about which parts you can research or which skills you need to practise more at home. You must write the report in the class, but you can reflect upon what needs to be done and make brief notes at home.

## AVOID STRESS

It is very easy to feel stressed in the run-up to the exams. There are steps that you can take to reduce stress and improve your performance.

Exercise releases tension and takes your mind off the issues that are stressing you. You do not need to run 10 miles. Even a short walk can have a relaxing and calming effect.

Try to make a peaceful study area for yourself which is quiet and free from distractions. It is very hard to study effectively in a family room with a loud TV on and your baby sister tugging your feet!

It is also important that you don't work too hard and overdo it. Studies have shown that relatively short periods of studying, each followed up with a short break, are more effective than working flat out for hours on end.

Remember that what you eat and drink also has an influence on how you feel and on your ability to concentrate. A healthy, well-balanced diet will put you in a much better state of mind for study than if you consume fizzy drinks and junk food.

**VIDEO**

Watch the clip on tackling assignments: www.brightredbooks.net/N5Computing

**ONLINE**

The SQA has a study guide section on its website which gives further support on how to prepare for and cope with exams. Enter the keywords 'SQA' and 'study guide' into a search engine to find this information.

## THINGS TO DO AND THINK ABOUT

Each year, the SQA produces an examiner's report, which can be found on its website. This report gives helpful comments on strong and weak areas of student performance and cut-off scores for each grade. This report can give you a useful insight into the exam process.

# GLOSSARY

**Absolute hyperlink**
An absolute hyperlink refers to the use of the complete URL.
Example: <a href="http://www.bbc.co.uk/weather.html">Click here</a>

**Address bus**
A processor bus that is used to specify which memory location is to be used to read data from or to write data to.

**Adware**
Software that irritatingly displays advertisements on a computer.

**ALU (Arithmetic Logic Unit)**
A component of the processor that performs arithmetic operations and logical decisions.

**Anchor**
A specific place within an HTML document to which a link is set to point.

**And**
A logical operator that requires both of two conditions to be true.

**Anti-virus software**
Software that scans a computer system to detect and remove viruses.

**Array**
A data structure that stores a list of items of the same data type.

**ASCII**
American Standard Code for Information Interchange. A system for storing characters on a computer system using an 8-bit code.

**Assignment**
The process of assigning a value to a variable.

**Audio**
An HTML tag, <audio>, that is used to define sound content in an HTML document.

**Background-color**
A CSS property that sets the background colour of an element.

**Binary**
A two-digit numerical system that computers use to represent data.

**Biometrics**
A form of security system based on the detection and recognition of human physical characteristics.

**Bit**
A binary digit (1 or 0).

**Bit depth**
The number of bits allocated for the colour code of each pixel.

**Bit-mapped**
A graphic where the image is stored as a binary code for the colour of pixels.

**BMP (Bitmap)**
A standard file format for graphics that uses a binary code to store the colour of each pixel.

**Body**
An HTML tag, <body>, that contains all the contents of an HTML document, such as text, hyperlinks, images, tables, lists and so on.

**Boolean**
A data type used for a variable that is storing only the values True or False.

**Boolean field**
A field that stores only two values (Yes or No).

**Browser**
A program that is used to display web pages and navigate around the internet.

**Byte**
A group of 8 bits.

**Calculation field**
A field whose contents are calculated by a formula using the other fields in a record.

**Carbon footprint**
A measure of how much carbon dioxide is produced in the manufacture and use of computing equipment.

**Character**
A data type used for a variable that is storing a single character.

**Class selector**
A selector that is used to define CSS rules that can be used with more than one element on the web page.

**Color**
A CSS property that sets the colour of text to a colour name, "red", a HEX value, "#ff0000" or an RGB value, "rgb(255,0,0)".

**Colour depth**
The number of bits allocated for the colour code of each pixel.

**Compiler**
A translator program which converts high-level language code into stand-alone machine code.

**Conditional loop**
A loop that repeats a set of instructions as often as is necessary until a condition is true.

**Conditional statement**
A statement that is either True or False.

**Control bus**
A processor bus that sends out signals along various lines to initiate events.

**Control character**
Non-printing characters such as RETURN and TAB.

**Control unit**
A component of the processor that manages the fetching and execution of instructions from main memory.

**Copyright, Designs and Patents Act (1988)**
An Act which covers the illegal copying of music, films, images, manuscripts etc. stored on a computer.

**CPU (Central Processing Unit)**
The part of a computer that executes programs and consists of a processor chip and main memory chips.

**CSS (Cascading Style Sheets)**
A system for defining the way a web page is formatted by using CSS rules to define the font, colour, size and alignment of text, the positions of images and so on.

**Database**
An organised collection of records.

**Data bus**
A processor bus that is used to carry data from a memory location to the processor and vice versa.

**Data Protection Act (1998)**
An Act to protect the rights of individuals in society against misuse of their data being held on computer systems.

**Data types**
Different kinds of data stored by a variable in a program, such as Integer, String, Boolean and so on.

**Date field**
A field that stores a date.

**Delete**
To remove data, especially removing a record from a database.

**Div**
An HTML tag, <div>, that is used to divide an HTML document into sections.

**Encryption**
Encoding data so that it cannot be interpreted if unlawfully accessed.

**End user**
The person/persons who will be using an item of software once it has been developed.

**Entity relationship diagram**
A diagram that represents the relationship between tables in a relational database by showing the links between the primary and foreign keys.

**Equi-join**
Combining the data from two tables in a relational database by selecting data where a primary key in one table is equal to a foreign key in another table.

**Exceptional data**
A set of test data that is chosen to test whether the software can deal with unexpected data without crashing.

**Execution errors**
Errors that are detected during the running of the program, such as dividing by zero.

**Exponent**
The power part of a floating-point number.

**External hyperlink**
A link to a web page or file stored in another website.

**External stylesheet**
CSS rules that are defined in a separate .CSS file with a link placed in the <head> section of the HTML document.

**Extreme data**
A set of test data that is chosen to test that the software can handle data which lies on the boundaries of possible data.

**Field**
An item of data in a database record.

**Field length check**
A validation check which forces the entered data to be a specified number of characters long.

**Fill colour**
The colour used to fill in a shape in a vector graphics program.

**Firewall**
Hardware and software that is used to protect a computer from damage by filtering all incoming and outgoing internet traffic.

**Fitness for purpose**
Software that fulfils the requirements and does what it is supposed to do.

**Fixed loop**
A loop that repeats a set of instructions a pre-determined number of times.

**Flat-file database**
A database that contains records in only one table of data.

**Floating-point notation**
A method of storing real numbers on a computer system.

**Flowchart**
A method of design that represents an algorithm by showing the steps as boxes of various kinds and their order by connecting them with arrows.

**Font-family**
A CSS property that specifies the font for an element. A list of fonts is given so that if the first font is not available, then the second font is used, and so on.

**Font-size**
A CSS property that sets the size of the font, typically specified in pixels.

**Foreign key**
A field that contains values that correspond to values in the primary key of another table.

**Frame rates**
The number of frames that are captured per second.

**Functional requirements**
The input, processing and output operations that a computer system is required to perform.

**GIF (Graphics Interchange Format)**
A standard file format for graphics that uses lossless compression and represents 256 colours.

**Gigabyte (GB)**
A gigabyte = $2^{30}$ bytes = 1,073,741,824 bytes.

**Graphics field**
A field that stores an image.

**Hacking**
Gaining access to private and confidential data on a computer system.

**Hardware**
The physical parts of a computer such as the keyboard, hard disc drive and so on.

**Head**
An HTML tag, <head>, that contains the title of the document, scripts, styles and so on.

**Heading**
An HTML tag that defines a decreasing size of heading from <h1> to <h6>.

**High-level language**
A programming language that uses English command words to make the process of software development easier and quicker.

**Home page**
The first web page that is displayed in a browser when a website is loaded.

**HTML (Hypertext Mark-up Language)**
A language that uses a list of tags to describe a web page's format and what is displayed on the page.

**Hyperlink**
A link in an information system to another item within the file or to a document outside the file.

**ID selector**
A selector that is used to define CSS rules that can be used with only one element on the web page.

**Img**
An HTML tag, <img>, that is used to define an image in an HTML document.

**Indentation**
Indenting instructions in the program code to make it easier to identify selection, looping and so on.

**Input validation**
The process of repeatedly asking for an item of data to be entered until it is within its possible range of values.

**Insert**
To add in data, especially adding a record to a database.

**Integer**
A data type used for a variable that is storing a positive or negative whole number.

**Internal commentary**
Comments inserted into a program listing to explain what the instructions are doing.

**Internal hyperlink**
A link to a web page or file stored within the same site.

**Internal stylesheet**
CSS rules that are defined within a <style> element in the <head> section of a page.

**Interpreter**
A translator program which converts high-level language code into machine code one instruction at a time when the program is run.

**Iteration**
The process where programs repeat a group of instructions two or more times.

**JavaScript**
A programming language that can be incorporated into web pages to add interactivity and make them more dynamic.

**JPEG (Joint Photographic Experts Group)**
A standard file format for graphics that uses lossy compression and represents over 16 million colours.

**Keylogger**
Software that records the keys that the user presses on a computer keyboard.

**Kilobyte (Kb)**
A kilobyte = $2^{10}$ bytes = 1,024 bytes.

**Line colour**
The colour used for the border of a shape in a vector graphics program.

**List – item**
An HTML tag, <li>, that is used to define a list item in an HTML document.

**List – ordered**
An HTML tag, <ol>, that is used to define an ordered list in an HTML document.

**List – unordered**
An HTML tag, <ul>, that is used to define an unordered list in an HTML document.

**Logical errors**
Errors caused by mistakes in the code that cause the program not to produce the correct results.

**Lossless compression**
File compression that results in no reduction in quality.

**Lossy compression**
File compression that reduces the quality of the file.

**Machine code**
The computer's own programming language where instructions and data are written in binary codes.

**Main memory**
Memory in the CPU that is used to store programs temporarily while they are being run.

**Mantissa**
The fractional part of a floating-point number which stores the significant figures of the number.

**Meaningful identifiers**
Variable names that relate to the data that the variable is storing.

**Megabyte (Mb)**
A megabyte = $2^{20}$ bytes = 1,048,756 bytes.

**MP3 (MPEG Layer 3)**
A standard file format for sound that uses lossy compression so that the quality is reduced.

**Multimedia**
A combination of text, graphics, video and sound data.

**Nested loop**
A loop which is placed completely inside another loop.

**Normal data**
A set of test data that is chosen to test that the software gives correct results for everyday data.

**Not**
A logical operator that switches a statement that is False to a statement that is True and vice versa.

**Numeric field**
A field that stores a number.

**Onmouseout**
A mouse event which triggers the execution of code when the mouse pointer is moved away from a specified element in a web page.

**Onmouseover**
A mouse event which triggers the execution of code when the mouse pointer is moved over a specified element in a web page.

**Operating system**
A large program that manages the hardware and software of a computing system.

**Or**
A logical operator that requires one of two conditions to be true.

**Paragraph**
A tag, <p>, that represents a paragraph of text.

**Petabyte (Pb)**
A petabyte = $2^{50}$ bytes = 1,125,899,906,842,624 bytes.

**Phishing**
The process of stealing private information through using false websites.

**Pixel**
A picture element; one of the tiny dots that make up a picture.

**PNG (Portable Network Graphics)**
A standard file format for graphics that uses lossless compression and represents over 16 million colours.

**Pre-defined function**
A function built into the programming language which performs mathematical calculations, manipulates text and so on.

**Presence check**
A validation check that is used to stop important data from being missed out, i.e. that will not allow a field to be left blank.

**Primary key**
A field that is used to uniquely identify each record in a table.

**Pseudocode**
A method of design that uses natural language to represent the detailed logic of the program code.

**RAM (Random-Access Memory)**
Part of main memory that can be read from and written to.

**Range check**
A validation check which forces the entered data to lie in a certain range of values.

**Readable**
Program code that is easily understood by another programmer.

**Real**
A data type used for a variable that is storing a positive or negative decimal number.

**Record**
Data on one person, animal or object in a database that consists of several fields.

**Referential integrity**
Avoiding inconsistencies by applying changes to a primary key in one table to all linked foreign keys in other tables.

**Registers**
Individual storage locations on the processor that store single items of data.

**Relational database**
A database that contains records in two or more linked tables.

**Relative hyperlink**
A relative hyperlink uses a path from the current page to the destination page.
Example: <a href="weather.html">Click here</

**Resolution**
The size of the pixels in an image, usually described in dots per inch (d.p.i.).

**Restricted choice**
A validation check that limits what the user can enter by restricting their choice to a list of acceptable values.

**Robust**
Describes software that does not crash easily with unexpected input.

**ROM (Read-Only Memory)**
Part of main memory that can be read from but not written to.

**Sample size**
The number of bits used to store each sound sample.

**Sampling rate**
The number of times that the sound is sampled per second.

**Scripting language**
A language that operates alongside an application package and allows the user to customise the package and to automate tasks.

**Searching**
Selecting records in a database according to certain rules based on one or more fields.

**Security suite**
A group of utility programs that protect a computer from viruses and other malware.

**Selection**
A programming construct where different sets of instructions are chosen to allow the program to make decisions.

**Sequencing**
A programming construct where the instructions are executed one after another.

**Software**
Computer programs such as Windows, Excel and so on.

**Sorting**
Arranging the records in a database into ascending or descending order.

**Spyware**
Software that, once installed on your computer, can 'spy' on your activities.

**SQL (Structured Query Language)**
A programming language that is used to manage the data in a database by selecting, updating, inserting and deleting data.

**Standard algorithms**
Common algorithms that are used in programs over and over again.

**Standard file format**
A file format that is recognised by a variety of software packages.

**Stand-by**
A low-power state which keeps the computer's data in memory while other parts of the computer are switched off.

**String**
A data type used for a variable that is storing an item of text.

**Structure diagram**
A method of design that splits a program into successively smaller and more manageable parts in a hierarchical structure.

**Syntax errors**
Errors which result from mistakes in the instructions of a programming language.

**Tablet computer**
A flat portable computer that is larger than a smartphone and smaller than a laptop, which uses a touchscreen for input rather than a physical keyboard.

**Tags**
Commands that are used to describe a web page by identifying elements on the page such as a header, title, body and so on.

**Terabyte (Tb)**
A terabyte = $2^{40}$ bytes = 1,099,511,627,776 bytes.

**Test data**
Sets of data chosen to detect and remove errors in a program.

**Text-align**
A CSS property that specifies the horizontal alignment of text in an element.

**Text field**
A field that stores a string of characters.

**Time field**
A field that stores a time of day.

**Title**
An HTML tag, <title>, that contains the page title which is displayed in the browser toolbar.

**Two-state**
A system that has only two states, for example a switch that is off or on.

**Two's complement**
A system for storing integers on a computer.

**Uniform Resource Locator**
A unique address that specifies a web page by the protocol, the domain name, the path to the file and the name of the file.

**Update**
To amend data, especially amending a record in a database.

**User interface**
A term used to describe how the user communicates with a computer program.

**Variable**
A label for an item of data that is stored in a program.

**Vector graphics**
A graphic where the image is stored as a list of objects and their attributes.

**Video**
An HTML tag, <video>, that is used to define video content in an HTML document.

**Virus**
A program which causes damage to a computer system and can replicate and spread to other computers.

**WAV (Waveform Audio Format)**
A standard file format for sound that uses lossless compression.

**White space**
Blank areas in the program listing, such as blank lines between control constructs and procedures and indentation in loops and IFs.

**Wireframe**
A skeletal illustration of a user interface showing the positioning of elements on the screen.

**World-Wide Web (WWW)**
The vast amount of multimedia information stored on websites on server computers on the internet.